THE UK
KETO DIET
Book for Women Over 50

The Ultimate Beginners Keto Diet
Cookbook to Boost the Immune System
with Easy to Make and Delcious Recipes

INCL. SPECIAL KETO DIET PLAN

OLIVIA C. SMITH

ISBN: 9798794776706

Table of Contents

INTRODUCTION

The keto diet is so different from other weight loss diet plans that it tends to spark concern, particularly regarding women's health.

There is no doubt that carb restriction can promote substantial amounts of fat loss for many women, but its impact on hormone levels, fertility, pregnancy, and menopause is often misunderstood.

This naturally begs the question: Do keto weight loss results come at a cost, or is the diet a win-win for women's health? To help answer this critical question, we've developed this comprehensive guide to keto for women.

What is Keto Diet?

A keto diet is a restrictive eating style that changes the type of fuel your body uses. The diet starves the body of glucose, the main source of energy that comes from carbohydrates. Legumes, bread, pasta, cereal, starchy vegetables like potatoes, dairy foods and sweets aren't typically on the menu.

Without glucose, the liver transforms stored fat into chemicals called ketone bodies, which are then consumed by the brain and body as energy.

To fuel ketosis, the body needs more fat, which is why a **classic keto diet** includes:

- 90% of calories from fat (especially saturated fat such as red meat, whipping cream and butter).
- 6% of calories from protein (too much protein throws a monkey wrench into ketosis).
- 4% of calories from carbohydrates.

Modified keto diets typically include less fat, more protein and often more carbohydrates than a classic keto diet. The ratios vary widely, depending on the diet:

- 70% to 87% of calories from fat.
- 10% to 15% of calories from protein.
- 3% to 15% of calories from carbs.

"Both the classic keto and modified keto diets are far from how most people normally eat. The majority of our calories – around 45% to 65% – come from carbs normally. These diets drive the carbs down to around 10% and limit so many food groups that it becomes almost impossible to follow this eating pattern long term," says Liz Weinandy, the lead outpatient registered dietitian at Ohio State University Wexner Medical Center.

What is Ketosis?

Ketosis is a metabolic state in which there's a high concentration of ketones in the blood. This happens when fat provides most of the fuel for the body, and there's limited access to glucose. Glucose (blood sugar) is the preferred fuel source for many cells in the body.

Ketosis is most often associated with ketogenic and very low carb diets. It also happens during pregnancy, infancy, fasting and starvation.

For ketosis to start, you generally need to eat fewer than 50 grams of carbs per day and sometimes as little as 20 grams per day. However, the exact carb intake that will cause ketosis varies between individuals.

To do this, you may need to remove certain food items from your diet, such as:

- grains
- candy
- sugary soft drinks

You also have to cut back on:

- legumes
- potatoes
- fruit

When eating a very low carb diet, levels of the hormone insulin go down and fatty acids are released from body fat stores in large amounts.

Many of these fatty acids are transported to the liver, where they're oxidized and turned into ketones (or ketone bodies). These molecules can provide energy for the body.

Unlike fatty acids, ketones can cross the blood-brain barrier and provide energy for the brain in the absence of glucose.

Is Keto Safe, Healthy, and Effective for All Women?

According to the research literature and the abundance of success stories, the keto diet can be a safe and effective weight loss approach that helps improve many common women's health struggles.

The keto diet may be most effective for women who are struggling with:

- Weight loss and yo-yo dieting
- Epilepsy
- Polycystic ovarian syndrome (PCOS)
- Yeast overgrowth

- Insulin resistance, type 1 diabetes, or type 2 diabetes
- Heart disease
- Neurodegenerative diseases such as Alzheimer's or Parkinson's
- Certain forms of cancer

That being said, some groups of women may find a different low-carb approach to be better for their overall health. This may include women who are:

- Female athletes/lifters that notice a significant drop in performance and recovery on keto 2-3 months.
- Struggling with a hypothyroid condition that isn't responding well to keto.
- Notice a worsening in blood lipid levels when they eat high amounts of saturated fat.
- Gain fat on a keto diet after tracking macros
- Have stopped menstruating or are having an irregular cycle
- Are pregnant or breastfeeding before their body has adapted to keto
- Notice an increase in menopause-related symptoms after 2-3 months of keto

Regardless of your current health condition, we must also keep in mind that the success of any diet depends significantly on the person. It will take some self-experimentation before you find out what approach to keto is the right fit for you.

Although this implies there will be some ups and downs along the way, this also means that you are not destined to be less healthy and gain fat as you age. Even if you are over 50 and struggling with menopause, you will still be able to achieve your health and weight loss goals.

Keto and weight loss for women

One of the main reasons why women turn to the keto diet is to lose excess body fat.

Some research suggests the keto diet may be an effective way to encourage fat loss in the female population.

Studies have shown that following a keto diet may aid weight loss by increasing fat burning and decreasing calorie intake and hunger-promoting hormones like insulin — all of which may help encourage fat loss.

For example, one study in 45 women with ovarian or endometrial cancer found that women who followed a ketogenic diet for 12 weeks had significantly less total body fat and lost 16% more belly fat than women assigned to a low fat, high fiber diet.

Another study in adults with obesity that included 12 women demonstrated that following a very low-calorie ketogenic diet for 14 weeks significantly reduced body fat, decreased food cravings, and improved female sexual function.

Additionally, a review of 13 randomized controlled trials — the gold standard in research — that included a population comprised of 61% women found that participants who followed ketogenic diets lost 2 pounds (0.9 kg) more than those on low fat diets after 1 to 2 years.

Although research supports the use of this very low carb way of eating to enhance fat loss in the short term, keep in mind that there's currently a lack of studies exploring the long-term effects of the keto diet on weight loss.

Plus, some evidence suggests that the weight-loss-promoting benefits of the keto diet drop off around the 5-month mark, which may be due to its restrictive nature.

What's more, some research shows that less restrictive low carb diets may result in comparable effects and are easier to sustain long term.

For example, a study that included 52 women found that low and moderate carb diets that contained 15% and 25% carbs, respectively, reduced body fat and waist circumference over 12 weeks similar to a ketogenic diet that contained 5% carbs.

Plus, the higher carb diets were easier for the women to stick to.

Does Keto Work for Middle-Aged Women?

There is a lot of research to substantiate the efficacy of keto for women over 50, but most of it is not geared toward its usefulness for losing weight. Researchers and even doctors recommend keto diets to treat various ailments and conditions, but little scientific research has studied its effects on weight loss.

However, there is an abundance of circumstantial evidence to support that a keto diet can help you lose weight, even when you're over 50.

When you restrict carbohydrate intake and maintain a state of ketogenesis, your body naturally turns to fat as its primary source of energy. If you also maintain a caloric deficit while on a keto diet, your fat stores will be the primary target for fuel instead of carbohydrates, ultimately leading to weight loss.

As such, many people who struggle to burn that stubborn belly fat find that a keto diet works wonders to prepare their bodies to pull energy from their stored fat.

A study published in the Journal of Women's Health found that keto for women over 50 is safe and effective and can aid in weight loss. The study involved over 65 women averaging 54 years old. After 12 weeks of following a strict ketogenic diet and eating at a caloric deficit, 60% of the participants lost at least 10% of their body weight.

Does Keto Cause Menopause?

Keto and menopause – two words women might not connect as they reach the transition that ends most estrogen production, menstrual cycles and the reproductive years. But keto and menopause are getting lots of attention now that the ketogenic or keto diet has become a popular eating style. "The keto diet has been around for a long time, and there are certain benefits for menopausal women. But there are many downsides, too," says Dr. Michael Tahery, an obstetrician and urogynecologist based in Los Angeles.

Keto and Menopause: Benefits

Some people turn to keto for menopause to address physical changes and menopause symptoms. For example, without estrogen, metabolism slows and the body redistributes fat. "Weight collects in the abdomen, even if there hasn't been weight gain," Tahery notes.

Falling estrogen levels also cause menopause symptoms that can last up to seven years including:

- Hot flashes and night sweats.
- Mood changes.
- Fatigue.
- Difficulty sleeping.
- Fuzzy thinking.
- Vaginal dryness.

Theoretically, the fat-rich ketogenic diet may reduce some menopause symptoms. "Fat is a precursor for estrone, a weak type of estrogen produced by fat cells," Tahery says. "The more fat you consume, the more estrogen you'll have in your system. It may contribute to fewer hot flashes, mood changes and fatigue."

Keto may help you:

- Lose weight, reducing your risk for developing heart disease, joint problems and cancer.
- Reduce blood glucose levels, reducing the risk for Type 2 diabetes.
- Improve insulin sensitivity, making this hormone that shepherds glucose to cells more effective.

However, it's important to note that the benefits of keto and menopause are believed to be short-term only. Weight loss, for example, may be the result of losing fluids as sugar stores in the body are emptied. "The keto diet acts as a diuretic," Weinandy says.

You may regain the weight as soon as you go off the diet, if you don't exercise or reduce the amount of calories you consume.

5 Natural Ways to Lower Your Cholesterol Levels

Cholesterol is made in your liver and has many important functions. For example, it helps keep the walls of your cells flexible and is needed to make several hormones.
However, like anything in the body, too much cholesterol or cholesterol in the wrong places creates problems.

Like fat, cholesterol does not dissolve in water. Instead, its transport in the body depends on molecules called lipoproteins, which carry cholesterol, fat and fat-soluble vitamins in the blood.

Different kinds of lipoproteins have different effects on health. For example, high levels of low-density lipoprotein (LDL) result in cholesterol deposits in blood vessel walls, which can lead to clogged arteries, strokes, heart attacks and kidney failure.

In contrast, high-density lipoprotein (HDL) helps carry cholesterol away from vessel walls and helps prevent these diseases.

This article will review 10 natural ways to increase the "good" HDL cholesterol and lower the "bad" LDL cholesterol.

1. Focus on Monounsaturated Fats

As opposed to saturated fats, unsaturated fats have at least one double chemical bond that changes the way they are used in the body. Monounsaturated fats have only one double bond.

Although some recommend a low-fat diet for weight loss, a study of 10 men found a 6-week, low-fat diet reduced levels of harmful LDL, but also reduced beneficial HDL.

In contrast, a diet high in monounsaturated fats reduced harmful LDL, but also protected higher levels of healthy HDL.

A study of 24 adults with high blood cholesterol came to the same conclusion, where eating a diet high in monounsaturated fat increased beneficial HDL by 12%, compared to a diet low in saturated fat.

Monounsaturated fats may also reduce the oxidation of lipoproteins, which contributes to clogged arteries. A study of 26 people found that replacing polyunsaturated fats with monounsaturated fats in the diet reduced the oxidation of fats and cholesterol.

Overall, monounsaturated fats are healthy because they decrease harmful LDL cholesterol, increase good HDL cholesterol and reduce harmful oxidation.

Here are a few great sources of monounsaturated fats. Some are also good sources of polyunsaturated fat:

- Olives and
- olive oil
- Canola oil
- Tree nuts, such as almonds, walnuts,
- pecans, hazelnuts and cashews
- Avocados

2. Avoid Trans Fats

Trans fats are unsaturated fats that have been modified by a process called hydrogenation. This is done to make the unsaturated fats in vegetable oils more stable as an ingredient. Many margarines and shortenings are made of partially hydrogenated oils.

The resulting trans fats are not fully saturated, but are solid at room temperatures. This is why food companies have used trans fats in products like spreads, pastries and cookies — they provide more texture than unsaturated, liquid oils.

Unfortunately, partially hydrogenated trans fats are handled differently in the body than other fats, and not in a good way. Trans fats increase total cholesterol and LDL, but decrease beneficial HDL by as much as 20%.

A study of global health patterns estimated trans fats may be responsible for 8% of deaths from heart disease worldwide. Another study estimated a law restricting trans fats in New York will reduce heart disease deaths by 4.5%.

In the United States and an increasing number of other countries, food companies are required to list the amount of trans fats in their products on nutrition labels.

However, these labels can be misleading, because they are allowed to round down when the amount of trans fat per serving is less than 0.5 grams. This means some foods contain trans fats even though their labels say "0 grams of trans fat per serving."

To avoid this trick, read the ingredients in addition to the nutrition label. If a product contains "partially hydrogenated" oil, it has trans fats and should be avoided.

3. Eat Soluble Fiber

Soluble fiber is a group of different compounds in plants that dissolve in water and that humans can't digest.

However, the beneficial bacteria that live in your intestines can digest soluble fiber. In fact, they require it for their own nutrition. These good bacteria, also called probiotics, reduce both harmful kinds of lipoproteins, LDL and VLDL.

In a study of 30 adults, taking 3 grams of soluble fiber supplements daily for 12 weeks decreased LDL by 18%.

A different study of fortified breakfast cereal found that added soluble fiber from pectin reduced LDL by 4% and fiber from psyllium reduced LDL by 6%.

Soluble fiber can also help increase the cholesterol benefits of taking a statin medication. One 12-week study had 68 adults add 15 grams of the psyllium product Metamucil to their daily 10-mg dose of the lipid-lowering medication simvastatin. This was found to be as effective as taking a larger 20-mg dose of the statin without fiber.

Soluble fiber's benefits reduce the risk of disease. A large review of several studies found high fiber intakes of both soluble and insoluble fiber reduced the risk of death over 17 years by nearly 15%.

Another study of over 350,000 adults found those eating the most fiber from grains and cereals lived longer, and they were 15–20% less likely to die during the 14-year study.

Some of the best sources of soluble fiber include beans, peas and lentils, fruit, oats and whole grains. Fiber supplements like psyllium are also safe and inexpensive sources.

4. Lose weight

Dieting influences the way your body absorbs and produces cholesterol.

A two-year study of 90 adults on one of three randomly assigned weight loss diets found weight loss on any of the diets increased the absorption of cholesterol from the diet and decreased the creation of new cholesterol in the body.

Over these two years, "good" HDL increased while "bad" LDL did not change, thus reducing the risk of heart disease.

In another similar study of 14 older men, "bad" LDL decreased as well, providing even more heart protection.

A study of 35 young women showed decreased creation of new cholesterol in the body during weight loss over six months.

5. Try supplements

There is strong evidence that fish oil and soluble fiber improve cholesterol and promote heart health. Another supplement, coenzyme Q10, is showing promise in improving cholesterol, although its long-term benefits are not yet known.

Overall, weight loss has a double benefit on cholesterol by increasing beneficial HDL and decreasing harmful LDL.

10 Science-Based Ways to Reduce Hunger and Appetite

To lose weight, you generally need to reduce your daily calorie intake.

Unfortunately, weight loss diets often lead to increased appetite and severe hunger.

This can make it extremely difficult to lose weight and keep it off.

Here is a list of 10 science-based ways to reduce excessive hunger and appetite:

1. Eat Enough Protein

Adding more protein to your diet can increase feelings of fullness, make you eat less at your next meal and help you lose fat.

For instance, a weight loss study compared two breakfasts identical in calories: one consisting of eggs, the other of bagels.

Participants who had the egg breakfast lost 65% more weight and 16% more body fat over the eight-week study period.

In addition, a high protein intake may help to prevent muscle loss when daily calories are reduced for weight loss.

Making protein about 20–30% of your total calorie intake, or 0.45-0.55 g/lb of body weight (1.0–1.2 g/kg), seems sufficient to provide the benefits

2. Sleep Can Suppress Appetite and Stop Weight Gain

Making sure you get enough quality sleep can help suppress appetite.
Studies have been conducted that show sleep deprivation can cause an increase in hunger by as much as 24 percent. It may also decrease some fullness hormones by as much as 26 percent, CNN and Medical News Today report.
Research from the European Journal of Clinical Nutrition has shown that consumers who sleep fewer than seven hours nightly rate after-breakfast fullness levels as 26 percent lower.
Also, several studies (see Harvard T.H. Chan School of Public Health, The National Sleep Foundation, Current Opinion in Clinical Nutrition & Metabolic Care) have linked short sleep duration (less than six hours per night) with a 55 percent increase in the potential for obesity.
The Bottom Line: Those who get fewer than seven hours of sleep nightly are more likely to have increased hunger levels throughout the day.

3. Drink Coffee

Coffee has many benefits for health and sports performance — and may also help decrease your appetite.
Research shows that coffee increases the release of peptide YY (PYY). This hormone is produced in the gut in response to eating and promotes a feeling of fullness.
Scientists believe that PYY levels play an important role in determining how much you're likely to eat.
Interestingly, decaffeinated coffee may produce the highest reduction in hunger, with effects that last up to three hours after consumption.
However, more studies are required to pinpoint exactly how this works.

4. Water Can Give You a Feeling of Fullness

Having a glass of water before meals can help decrease the feelings of hunger you experience before mealtime.
Drinking water can also help you feel fuller quicker after meals and increase weight loss success, Time Magazine writes.
Studies in the European Journal of Nutrition have shown people who drink two glasses of water as soon as they finish eating a meal tend to consume 22 percent fewer calories than those who do not drink any water.
Scientists think that approximately 17 ounces of water are enough to stretch the stomach sufficiently for signals of fullness to reach the brain.
Water empties from the stomach quickly, so for this method to be successful, you must consume the water fairly close to mealtime.
It is possible if you start your meal with a bowl of soup as it will work the same way.

Researchers noted that when a person eats a bowl of soup right before a meal, there is a decrease in the hunger and reduction of approximately 100 calories from the meal itself.
The Bottom Line: A person who drinks low-calorie liquids before a meal can help you consume fewer calories and suppress appetite.

5. Eat Mindfully

Under normal conditions, your brain knows whether you're hungry or full.
However, eating quickly or while you're distracted can make it more difficult for your brain to recognize these signals.
Solve this problem by eliminating distractions and focusing on the foods in front of you — a key aspect of mindful eating.
Research shows that practicing mindfulness during meals can help people experience more pleasure while eating. This can help keep the focus on quality rather than quantity, and reduces binge eating behavior.
There also seems to be a link between hunger, fullness and what your eyes see.
One experiment offered two identical milkshakes to participants. One was called a "620-calorie indulgence," while the other was given a "120-calorie sensible" label.
Although both groups consumed the same amount of calories, hunger hormone levels dropped more for those who believed they drank the "indulgent" drink.
Believing that a drink contains more calories can also activate the brain areas linked to feeling full.
How full you feel may be influenced by what you see, and paying attention to what you eat can be very beneficial.

6. Add Spices to Your Meals

Ginger is not necessarily the only spice used to suppress appetite.
A recent review compared the effects of capsaicin and capsiate.
The results showed both had a positive effect and helped fight hunger, WebMD reports.
The Bottom Line: The compounds found in hot and sweet peppers, like cayenne, can help curb hunger and increase the sense of fullness.

7. Eat on Smaller Plates

Reducing the size of your dinnerware can help you unconsciously reduce your meal portions. This is likely to help you consume less food without feeling deprived.
Interestingly, this effect can fool even the most aware eater.
For instance, a study observed that even nutrition experts unconsciously served themselves 31% more ice cream when given larger bowls.
Research has shown that when you have more on your plate, you're likely to eat more without realizing it.

8. Get Enough Sleep

Getting enough quality sleep can also help reduce hunger and protect against weight gain. Studies show that too little sleep can increase hunger and appetite by up to 24%, and decrease levels of some fullness hormones by up to 26%.

Research also shows that individuals who sleep less than seven hours per night rate their fullness levels after breakfast as 26% lower.

It's worth noting that several studies also link short sleep, generally defined as less than six hours per night, with up to a 55% higher risk of obesity

9. Reduce Your Stress

Excess stress is known to raise levels of the hormone cortisol.

Although the effects can vary between individuals, high cortisol is generally thought to increase food cravings and the drive to eat.

Stress may also decrease levels of peptide YY (PYY), a fullness hormone.

In a recent experiment, participants ate an average of 22% more calories after a stressful test when compared to a non-stressful version of the same test.

Finding ways to reduce your stress levels may not only help curb hunger, but also reduce your risk of obesity and depression

10. Exercise

Exercise is thought to reduce the activation of brain regions linked to food cravings, which can result in a lower motivation to eat.

It can also reduce hunger hormone levels, while increasing feelings of fullness.

Research shows that aerobic and resistance exercise are equally effective at influencing hormone levels and the size of a meal eaten after exercise.

Benefits of keto diet?

The ketogenic diet actually originated as a tool for treating neurological diseases such as epilepsy.

Studies have now shown that the diet can have benefits for a wide variety of different health conditions:

Heart disease: The ketogenic diet can help improve risk factors like body fat, HDL (good) cholesterol levels, blood pressure, and blood sugar.

Cancer: The diet is currently being explored as an additional treatment for cancer, because it may help slow tumor growth.

Alzheimer's disease: The keto diet may help reduce symptoms of Alzheimer's disease and slow its progression.

Epilepsy: Research has shown that the ketogenic diet can cause significant reductions in seizures in epileptic children.

Parkinson's disease: Although more research is needed, one study found that the diet helped improve symptoms of Parkinson's disease.

Polycystic ovary syndrome: The ketogenic diet can help reduce insulin levels, which may play a key role in polycystic ovary syndrome.

Brain injuries: Some research suggests that the diet could improve outcomes of traumatic brain injuries.

How does it help immune system?

A study was conducted recently where the researchers fed the Keto diet (low-carb, high-fat diet) to a group of mice who were infected with flu virus. The report revealed that the group of mice who were given Keto diet showed higher rate of survival in comparison to the group that was on regular high-carb diet. The researchers found that the Keto one led to release of immune-system cells which produce mucus around lung cell linings. The mucus produced helped to trap the flu virus on time before it could get worse.

According to the researchers, inflammasomes (activators of immune system) can lead to harmful responses in immune system of the host. The great news is, Ketogenic diet is able to prevent formation of these unwanted inflammasomes which eventually helps to strengthen immunity.

Does Keto Diet have any health risks?

A ketogenic diet has numerous risks. Top of the list: it's high in saturated fat. McManus recommends that you keep saturated fats to no more than 7% of your daily calories because of the link to heart disease. And indeed, the keto diet is associated with an increase in "bad" LDL cholesterol, which is also linked to heart disease.

Other potential keto risks include these:

Nutrient deficiency: "If you're not eating a wide variety of vegetables, fruits, and grains, you may be at risk for deficiencies in micronutrients, including selenium, magnesium, phosphorus, and vitamins B and C," McManus says.

Liver problems: With so much fat to metabolize, the diet could make any existing liver conditions worse.

Kidney problems: The kidneys help metabolize protein, and McManus says the keto diet may overload them. (The current recommended intake for protein averages 46 grams per day for women, and 56 grams for men).

Constipation: The keto diet is low in fibrous foods like grains and legumes.

Fuzzy thinking and mood swings. "The brain needs sugar from healthy carbohydrates to function. Low-carb diets may cause confusion and irritability," McManus says.

Those risks add up — so make sure that you talk to a doctor and a registered dietitian before ever attempting a ketogenic diet.

Is Keto Diet a heart-healthy diet?

Low-carb diets like keto may have some heart health benefits. A systematic review of randomized controlled trials comparing low-carb and low-fat diets in overweight and obese patients looked at outcomes for nearly 1,800 patients in 17 studies with short-term (less than one year) follow-up. Low-carb diets were associated with significantly greater weight reduction and significantly lower predicted risk of heart disease tied to hardening of the arteries than low-fat diets, according to the study published October 2015 in the journal PLOS One.

Dr. Eric Westman, director of the Duke Lifestyle Medicine Clinic and an expert in low-carb and keto diets, recommends the keto diet for some of his patients with heart disease. That, he says, is because the metabolic syndrome – a cluster of symptoms including high triglycerides and low "good" HDL cholesterol, high blood pressure, and high blood sugar, linked to heart disease and diabetes – is caused by a diet that's high in processed carbs and low in healthy fats. He sees improved triglyceride and HDL levels in patients on the keto diet.

Other heart risk factors like high blood pressure may improve on the keto diet. However, anyone with an existing heart condition that goes on a diet should be monitored by their health care providers.

Can Keto Diet prevent or control diabetes?

Research suggests that people with type 2 diabetes can slim down and lower their blood sugar levels with the keto diet. In one study, people with type 2 lost weight, needed less medication, and lowered their A1c when they followed the keto diet for a year.
If you're insulin resistant - which means you have higher blood sugar levels because your body isn't responding properly to the hormone insulin -- you could benefit from nutritional ketosis, because your body will need and make less insulin.

There are fewer studies looking at the keto diet for people with type 1 diabetes. One small study found that it helped people with type 1 lower their A1c levels, but we need a lot more research to get the full picture of the diet's effects.

Keep in mind that most studies have only looked at the short-term results of the keto diet. It's unclear if it works as a long-term way to manage your diabetes.

If you decide to try the keto diet, be aware that it may be hard to stick to. The very low amount of carbs in the plan is a big change for many people. It also can make you feel tired for a few weeks until your body adapts. To make it a success, it's a good idea to make a meal plan you can follow, including keto-friendly meals and snacks to keep on hand.

Does Keto Diet allow for restrictions and preferences?

Most people can customize the Keto diet according to their needs. Check individual preferences for more information.

Supplement recommended?

A daily vitamin with minerals, including potassium and magnesium, can fill in potential gaps while following keto.

Vegetarian or Vegan: It's possible to adapt the keto diet for vegetarians or vegans, but it's more challenging. Keto-vegan and vegetarian recipes are available on the Healthful Pursuit site.

Gluten-Free: Yes. The keto diet already avoids high-gluten, high-carb foods such as wheat bread, cookies, and pasta. Many nut butter, a keto staple, are also gluten-free.

Low-Salt: Keto can lend itself to a low-salt approach if you avoid processed meats such as sausage and bacon.

Kosher: Yes. Kosher-keto recipes are available in cookbooks and on Facebook.

Halal: It's up to you to prepare meals within guidelines.

What types of meals should you eat on the Keto Diet?

If you crave fat, you're in luck. Start your day with a double "rocket fuel" latte, if you like – and don't skimp on the cacao butter. Lunch on ground turkey patties with a side of slaw or a couple of sausage links. Keto is one diet where you're encouraged to bypass leaner ground beef and dig into fatty chicken thighs instead of skinless breasts.

Prefer to go meatless? That's entirely possible, especially if you concentrate on low-carb veggies. Slather on some mayo for a tasty fat boost. As you become more comfortable, you may find yourself experimenting with exotic vegetable choices like kohlrabi. If you include fish-based meals, fattier fish like salmon will help meet keto requirements for moderate protein and high fat.

Keto Acceptable Food List

PROTEIN

- Bacon
- Beef
- Beef Jerky
- Bison
- Cheese
- Chicken
- Cottage Cheese
- Deer
- Deli Meat
- Duck
- Elk
- Goat
- Goose
- Hot Dogs
- Lamb
- Moose
- Pepperoni
- Pheasant
- Quail
- Rabbit
- Salami
- Sausages
- Sheep
- Turkey
- Veal
- Wild Boar
- Wild Turkey

FAT

- Avocado
- Avocado Oil
- Blue Cheese
- Brie
- Butter
- Cocoa Butter
- Coconut Butter
- Coconut Oil
- Red Palm Oil
- Salad Dressing
- Cream Cheese
- Duck Fat
- Egg Yolks
- Ghee
- Half and Half
- Lard
- Macadamia Oil
- MCT Oil
- Olive Oil
- Palm shortening
- Sesame Oil
- Tallow
- Walnut Oil
- Whole cream

NUTS & SEEDS

- Almonds
- Brazil Nuts
- Chia Seeds
- Hazelnuts
- Hemp Seeds
- Macadamia Nuts
- Peanuts
- Pecans
- Pine Nuts
- Walnuts
- Pistachios
- Nut Butters
- Sesame Seeds
- Tahini (Sesame Butter)
- Pumpkin Seeds
- Sunflower Seeds

FISH/ SEAFOOD

- Anchovies
- Bass
- Cod
- Eel
- Flounder
- Grouper
- Haddock
- Halibut
- Herring

- Mackerel
- Mahi-mahi
- Orange Roughy
- Perch
- Red Snapper
- Rockfish
- Salmon
- Sardines
- Tilapia
- Turbot
- Trout
- Tuna (Including
- Albacore)
- Sole
- Abalon
- Caviar
- Clams
- Crab
- Lobster
- Mussels
- Oysters
- Scallops
- Shrimps
- Squid
- Octopus

VEGETABLES

- Artichokes
- Arugula
- Asparagus
- Beet Greens
- Bok Choy
- Broccoli
- Brussels Sprouts
- Butterhead Lettuce
- Cabbage
- Carrots
- Cauliflower
- Celery
- Chard
- Chives
- Cucumber
- Dandelion Greens
- Eggplant
- Endives
- Fennel
- Garlic
- Green Beans
- Jicama
- Kale
- Kimchi
- Kohlrabi
- Leeks
- Leafy Greens
- Mushrooms (All kinds)
- Mustard Greens
- Okra
- Olive
- Onions
- Parsley
- Peppers (All kinds)
- Pumpkin
- Radicchio
- Radishes
- Rhubarb
- Sauerkraut
- Scallions
- Seaweed (All Sea Vegetables)
- Shallots
- Spaghetti Squash
- Spinach
- Swiss Chard
- Tomatoes
- Turnip Greens
- Watercress
- Zucchini
- Romaine Lettuce

BERRIES & FRUITS

- Blackberry
- Blueberry
- Cranberry
- Lemon
- Lime
- Olives
- Raspberry
- Strawberry

Will Keto Diet help you lose weight?

Recent studies focusing on keto diets suggest some advantages for short-term weight loss. It's still too soon to tell whether people maintain long-term weight loss from ketogenic diets.

In its 2016 report "Healthy Eating Guidelines & Weight Loss Advice," the Public Health Collaboration, a U.K. nonprofit, evaluated evidence on low-carbohydrate, high-fat diets. (The keto diet falls under the LCHF umbrella.) Among 53 randomized clinical trials comparing LCHF diets to calorie-counting, low-fat diets, a majority of studies showed greater weight loss for the keto-type diets, along with more beneficial health outcomes. The collaboration recommends weight-loss guidelines that include a low-carbohydrate, high-fat diet of real (rather than processed) foods as an acceptable, effective, and safe approach.

A small Feb. 20, 2017, study looked at the impact of a six-week ketogenic diet on physical fitness and body composition in 42 healthy adults. The study, published in the journal Nutrition & Metabolism, found a mildly negative impact on physical performance in endurance capacity, peak power, and faster exhaustion. Overall, researchers concluded, "Our findings lead us to assume that a [ketogenic diet] does not impact physical fitness in a clinically relevant manner that would impair activities of daily living and aerobic training." The "significant" weight loss of about 4.4 pounds, on average, did not affect muscle mass or function.

How easy is Keto Diet to follow?

If you love morning toast, whole-wheat pasta, pizza, and sugary desserts, you could struggle on the keto diet. You'll need time to prepare and educate yourself, and the first week won't be much fun.

How much should you exercise on Keto Diet?

To get the most benefit from the keto diet, you should stay physically active. You might need to take it easier during the early ketosis period, especially if you feel tired or lightheaded. Walking, running, doing aerobics, weightlifting, training with kettlebells, or whatever workout you prefer will further boost your energy. You can find books and online resources on how to adapt Keto meals or snacks for athletic training.

Is Keto Diet nutritious?

Experts had enough reservations to place the keto diet way down in this category with its combination of unusually high fat and remarkably low carb content. Experts expressed particular concern for people with liver or kidney conditions, who should avoid it altogether. The jury is still out whether Keto offers more potential health risks or benefits for people with heart conditions or diabetes. With the variety of Keto versions and food choices, and different cycling methods in and out of the diet, hormonal and other changes can vary widely.

Recipe Notes

We wanted to make it as simple as possible for you to get in the kitchen and rustle up something special, so you will find each recipe laid out in an easy to follow format. Remember this diet is designed to rekindle your love of food not extinguish it with rules and regulations, so don't be afraid to experiment.

Use the ingredients as general guidelines and follow the instructions as best you can. You may not get everything the perfect first time, every time but that is what makes it yours!

Keep at it for a full 30 days of eating and you will no doubt establish a few firm favourites that you can turn into your speciality dishes over time.

Each recipe ends with a breakdown of key nutritional information including the number of calories and amount of fats, carbohydrates and protein.

Again, this isn't to be obsessed over. Food is something to be enjoyed, so if you are going to keep a note of your intake levels then just make it a general estimate.

Why no pic? This cookbook is full of fun and flavour and doesn't take stuff too seriously. The food is entering your mouth, not a modelling contest, and we don't like to encourage unhealthy obsession about presentation. So just cook expert: tent, and enjoy.

Once you start loving what you are eating mealtimes will become something to look forward to. Take this as encouragement, go forth and cook to your heart's content!

Things to remember

A healthy diet is not a solution to anything In and of itself; it must be applied as part of a healthy lifestyle in order to see maximum results.

Think of the ketogenic diet as the foundation of your new body. If you want to build something truly special on top of it then design your lifestyle with that goal In mind.

Cutting out junk food goes without saying, as does ditching bad habits such as smoking and drinking. Exercise, too, wit take you to heights you never thought was possible.

So, as you explore these delectable dishes and embark on the keto diet, try not to neglect other areas of responsibility.

Let this be the start of something great!

28-Days Keto Diet Weight Loss Challenge

Now, the moment you've been waiting for — the meal plan! In this chapter, you'll find a 28-day meal plan for the standard ketogenic diet, divided into four weeks. Every day you'll follow the plan to eat breakfast, lunch, and dinner, as well as a snack or dessert with a calorie range between 1,800 and 2,000.

One thing I want to mention before you get started is net carbs.

Many people who follow the ketogenic diet prefer to track net carbs rather than total carbs. To calculate net carbs, you simply take the total carb count of the meal and subtract the grams of fiber since fiber cannot be digested. Personally. I prefer to track total carbs like what I have mentioned in my first book, but I have included the grams of fiber and net carbs in these recipes, so you can choose which way to go.

personally, l prefer more buffer when it comes to the carb count, because I want to reduce the number of obstacles keeping me from ketosis. Many of my readers as well as friends have raised this point and you can be sure quite a few nights or afternoons were spent in heated debate! Okay, it wasn't that serious but suffice it to say that quite a bit of discussion went into this topic Therefore, I thought it might be better if I gave you a say in this net carb-total carb debate. You get to choose whichever you prefer. In my personal opinion, when you are in the initial stages of trying to enter ketosis, keeping your total carb count in mind is probably one of the better practices you can adopt. A 20 to 50gram range of carbs would usually work to push the body into a ketogenic state.

After you have gotten keto adapted and the body gets used to burning fat for fuel, you on then start to bring net carbs into the equation.

Keep in mind the calorie range for these meal plans — if you read my first book and calculated your own daily caloric needs, you may need to make some adjustments. If you're trying the ketogenic diet for the first time, however, it may be easiest to just follow the plan as is until you get the hang of it.

The first week of this 28-day meal plan is designed to be incredibly simple in terms of meal prep so want can focus on learning which foods to eat and which to avoid on the ketogenic diet — that's why you'll find more smoothies and soups here than in the following weeks. If you finish the first week and feel like you still need some time making the adjustment to keto, feel free to repeat it before moving on to week two. The meal plans also take into account left-overs and the yields of various recipes, so that you have minimal wage from your efforts in the kitchen. So, without further ado, let's take a look at the meal plans

28-Days Keto Diet Weight Loss Challenge

First Week Meal Plan

Day	Breakfast	Lunch	Dinner
Sunday	Keto egg muffins (Page No. 31)	Special Bacon Sandwich (Page No. 58)	Grilled Chicken Thighs Rosemary (Page No. 66)
Monday	Keto Coffee (Page No. 45)	Blueberry Smoothie (Page No. 52)	Crispy Almond Chicken with Tomato (Page No. 79)
Tuesday	Bulletproof Coffee (Page No. 33)	Garlic Butter Chicken (Page No. 50)	Strawberries smoothie (Page No. 87)
Wednesday	Egg & Sausage Breakfast (Page No. 31)	Coconut Chicken Curry (Page No. 46)	Broccoli Cheddar Soup (Page No. 69)
Thursday	Chocolate Coconut Crunch Smoothie (Page No. 42)	Creamy Zucchini Noodles (Page No. 60)	Creamiest Chocolate Dessert (Page No. 83)
Friday	Blueberry Breakfast Smoothie (Page No. 37)	Cheese & Tomato Salad (Page No. 54)	Crispy Chicken with Cheese Sauce (Page No. 70)
Saturday	Egg on Avocado (Page No. 43)	Tantalizing Tuna & Spinach Mix (Page No. 49)	Chicken Avocado Creamy Salad (Page No. 73)

28-Days Keto Diet Weight Loss Challenge

Second Week Meal Plan

Day	Breakfast	Lunch	Dinner
Sunday	Blueberry Breakfast Smoothie (Page No. 37)	Cheese & Tomato Salad (Page No. 54)	Crispy Chicken with Cheese Sauce (Page No. 70)
Monday	Keto Coffee (Page No. 45)	Blueberry Smoothie (Page No. 52)	Crispy Almond Chicken with Tomato (Page No. 79)
Tuesday	Egg on Avocado (Page No. 43)	Tantalizing Tuna & Spinach Mix (Page No. 49)	Chicken Avocado Creamy Salad (Page No. 73)
Wednesday	Keto egg muffins (Page No. 31)	Special Bacon Sandwich (Page No. 59)	Grilled Chicken Thighs Rosemary (Page No. 66)
Thursday	Anti-Inflammatory Spice Smoothie (Page No. 42)	Egg Medley Muffins (Page No. 47)	Keto Blueberry Kefir Smoothie (Page No. 76)
Friday	Bulletproof Coffee (Page No. 33)	Garlic Butter Chicken (Page No. 50)	Strawberries smoothie (Page No. 87)
Saturday	Chocolate Coconut Crunch Smoothie (Page No. 42)	Creamy Zucchini Noodles (Page No. 60)	Creamiest Chocolate Dessert (Page No. 83)

28-Days Keto Diet Weight Loss Challenge

Third Week Meal Plan

Day	Breakfast	Lunch	Dinner
Sunday	Chocolate Coconut Crunch Smoothie (Page No. 42)	Creamy Zucchini Noodles (Page No. 60)	Creamiest Chocolate Dessert (Page No. 83)
Monday	Egg on Avocado (Page No. 43)	Tantalizing Tuna & Spinach Mix (Page No. 49)	Chicken Avocado Creamy Salad (Page No. 73)
Tuesday	Keto egg muffins (Page No. 31)	Blueberry Smoothie (Page No. 52)	Grilled Chicken Thighs Rosemary (Page No. 66)
Wednesday	Bulletproof Coffee (Page No. 33)	Egg Medley Muffins (Page No. 47)	Keto Blueberry Kefir Smoothie (Page No. 76)
Thursday	Anti-Inflammatory Spice Smoothie (Page No. 42)	Creamy Zucchini Noodles (Page No. 60)	Crispy Almond Chicken with Tomato (Page No. 79)
Friday	Keto Coffee (Page No. 45)	Special Bacon Sandwich (Page No. 58)	Broccoli Cheddar Soup (Page No. 69)
Saturday	Egg & Sausage Breakfast (Page No. 31)	Coconut Chicken Curry (Page No. 46)	Crispy Chicken with Cheese Sauce (Page No. 70)

28-Days Keto Diet Weight Loss Challenge

Fourth Week Meal Plan

Day	Breakfast	Lunch	Dinner
Sunday	Perfect Strawberry Pancakes (Page No. 34)	Egg Medley Muffins (Page No. 47)	Keto Blueberry Kefir Smoothie (Page No. 76)
Monday	Bulletproof Coffee (Page No. 33)	Creamy Zucchini Noodles (Page No. 60)	Creamiest Chocolate Dessert (Page No. 83)
Tuesday	Blueberry Breakfast Smoothie (Page No. 37)	Garlic Butter Chicken (Page No. 50)	Strawberries smoothie (Page No. 87)
Wednesday	Egg & Sausage Breakfast (Page No. 31)	Cheese & Tomato Salad (Page No. 54)	Crispy Chicken with Cheese Sauce (Page No. 70)
Thursday	Egg on Avocado (Page No. 43)	Coconut Chicken Curry (Page No. 46)	Broccoli Cheddar Soup (Page No. 69)
Friday	Keto egg muffins (Page No. 31)	Tantalizing Tuna & Spinach Mix (Page No. 49)	Chicken Avocado Creamy Salad (Page No. 73)
Saturday	Bulletproof Coffee (Page No. 33)	Blueberry Smoothie (Page No. 52)	Grilled Chicken Thighs Rosemary (Page No. 66)

Breakfast recipes

Egg & Sausage Breakfast

TIME TO PREPARE
5 Minutes

COOK TIME
45 Minutes

Serving
2 People

INGREDIENTS

- 12 eggs.
- 8 oz breakfast sausage.
- 8 oz cheddar cheese (grated).
- ¾ cup (180g) of thick cream or single cream.

- 1 tbsp onion (grated).
- 2 tsp mustard (powder).
- 1 tsp oregano (dried).

INSTRUCTIONS

1. Preheat oven at 350.
2. In a large frying pan, fry sausage for 6-7 minutes, breaking it with a fork as it cooks,
3. eventually looking like a crumble mixture. Spread into a casserole dish.
4. In a bowl, mix eggs, cheese, onion, oregano, mustard, and cream until well
5. combined. Pour over sausage mixture.
6. Bake for 35-40 minutes until thoroughly cooked.

Nutrition Per Serving: Calories: 375, Protein: 21 g, Fat: 32 g, Net Carbs: 2 g

Keto egg muffins

TIME TO PREPARE
10 Minutes

COOK TIME
25 Minutes

Serving
1 People

INGREDIENTS

- Two eggs
- 1/3 scallion, finely chopped
- One slice of air-dried chorizo or salami or cooked bacon

- 2 Tbsp shredded cheese
- 1 tsp red pesto or green pesto (optional)
- salt and pepper

INSTRUCTIONS

1. Preheat the oven to 350°F (175°C).

2. Grease a muffin tin thoroughly with butter.
3. Chop scallions and chorizo and add to the bottom of the tin.
4. Whisk eggs together with seasoning and pesto. Add the cheese and stir.
5. Pour the batter on top of the scallions and chorizo.
6. Bake for 15–20 minutes, depending on the size of the muffin tin.

Nutrition Per Serving: Calories: 336, Protein: 28 g, Fat: 70 g, Net Carbs: 2 g

Bacon & Broccoli Wrap

TIME TO PREPARE
5 Minutes

COOK TIME
5 Minutes

Serving
2 People

INGREDIENTS

- One large egg.
- One cup (150g) broccoli (chopped).
- One onion (sliced).
- One slice of bacon.
- ¼ cup tomatoes (chopped).

- 2 tbsp cheddar cheese.
- 1 tbsp milk.
- 1 tsp avocado oil.
- Pinch salt and pepper

INSTRUCTIONS

1. Fry bacon until crispy and remove from pan. Add broccoli and cook for 3 minutes until soft, mix in tomatoes and pour into a bowl.
2. In a separate bowl, mix egg, milk, onion, and salt and pepper. Add oil to a large frying
3. pan over medium heat; pour in the egg mixture, covering the frying pan's base. Cook for 2 minutes until the bottom has set, flip and cook the other side.
4. Place egg wrap on a plate, fill the bottom half with broccoli mixture, top with bacon, and roll into a wrap.

Nutrition Per Serving: Calories: 258, Protein: 15 g, Fat: 19 g, Net Carbs: 9 g

Avocado Coconut Milk Shake

TIME TO PREPARE
5 Minutes

COOK TIME
0 Minutes

Serving
1 People

INGREDIENTS

- ½ avocado
- ½ cups (120g) Unsweetened Coconut Milk
- 5 drops stevia
- 5 Ice Cubes

INSTRUCTIONS

1. Add all the ingredients to the blender.
2. Blend until smooth.

Nutrition Per Serving: Calories: 437, Protein: 4 g, Fat: 43 g, Net Carbs: 9 g

Bulletproof Coffee

TIME TO PREPARE
5 Minutes

COOK TIME
10 Minutes

Serving
1 People

INGREDIENTS

- 1 cup (250g) of water
- 2 tbsp coffee
- 1 tbsp grass-fed butter
- 1 tbsp coconut oil
- ¼ tsp vanilla extract

INSTRUCTIONS

1. Brew coffee your preferred way.
2. Add butter and coconut oil to the blender.
3. Pour the coffee into the blender.
4. Add the vanilla extract and blend for 20 seconds.

Nutrition Per Serving: Calories: 224, Protein: 16 g, Fat: 44 g, Net Carbs: 0.12 g

Cinnamon Chia Pudding

TIME TO PREPARE
3 Minutes

COOK TIME
00 Minutes

Serving
1 People

INGREDIENTS

- 1 tbsp chia seeds
- 1 cup (240ml) unsweetened almond milk
- ½ tsp ground cinnamon
- 1 tbsp peanut butter
- 8 drops stevia

INSTRUCTIONS

1. Add almond milk, peanut butter, cinnamon, and stevia to your blender.
2. Blend until smooth.
3. Add chia seeds to the mixture and stir.
4. Refrigerate for about 3 hours.
5. Enjoy!

Nutrition Per Serving: Calories: 384, Protein: 16 g, Fat: 24 g, Net Carbs: 10 g

Perfect Strawberry Pancakes

TIME TO PREPARE
5 Minutes

COOK TIME
15 Minutes

Serving
4 People

INGREDIENTS

- Four large eggs.
- 1 cup (240g) of thick cream or single cream.
- 7 oz cottage cheese.

- 2 oz fresh strawberries.
- 2 oz butter.
- 1 tbsp psyllium husk (powder).

INSTRUCTIONS

1. Mix cottage cheese, eggs, and psyllium husk until well combined. Allow resting for 10 minutes.
2. Heat butter in a large frying pan and fry each pancake on medium heat for 3-4 minutes on each side.

3. In a bowl, whip the cream until peaks are formed.
4. Serve the pancakes topped with cream and fresh strawberries.

Nutrition Per Serving: Calories: 324, Protein: 14 g, Fat: 40 g, Net Carbs: 4 g

Mixed Berry & Coconut Porridge

TIME TO PREPARE
10 Minutes

COOK TIME
00 Minutes

Serving
1 People

INGREDIENTS

- ½ cup (120g) almond milk.
- ¼ cup (70g) of mixed berries.
- ⅓ cup (80ml) of coconut milk.
- 2 tbsp flaxseed.
- 1 tbsp desiccated coconut.

- 1 tbsp almond meal.
- 1 tsp pumpkin seeds.
- ½ tsp cinnamon.
- ½ tsp vanilla extract.

INSTRUCTIONS

1. To a large saucepan, add coconut milk, almond milk, flaxseed, almond meal, coconut, cinnamon, and vanilla; stir continuously until mixture thickens.
2. Pour into a bowl and top with pumpkin seeds and mixed fruit.

Nutrition Per Serving: Calories: 444, Protein: 10 g, Fat: 40 g, Net Carbs: 6 g

Egg & Bacon Bakes

TIME TO PREPARE
5 Minutes

COOK TIME
15 Minutes

Serving
4 People

INGREDIENTS

- Six large eggs.
- Six bacon slices (chopped).
- 1 ½ cups (170g) cheddar cheese (grated).
- 6 tbsp salsa.
- 1 tbsp olive oil.

- 1 tsp black pepper.
- 1 tsp chili flakes.
- 1 tsp paprika.
- ½ tsp salt.

INSTRUCTIONS

1. Preheat the oven at 400 and line a baking sheet with greaseproof paper.
2. Split the cheese into six piles on the baking sheet.
3. Season the piles with paprika and chili flakes and bake for 10-11 minutes.
4. Place each cheese bake over an upside-down cup; allow to cool and mold itself to the shape. Set aside.
5. Heat the oil in a frying pan and fry the bacon until crispy. Remove bacon from the pan but leave the grease in the pan.
6. Heat the bacon grease and scramble six eggs, season with salt and pepper, and add to the cheese bakes.
7. Top each with 1 tbsp salsa and sprinkle each with bacon.

Nutrition Per Serving: Calories: 296, Protein: 16 g, Fat: 25 g, Net Carbs: 2 g

Stuffed Bacon Boats

TIME TO PREPARE
10 Minutes

COOK TIME
30 Minutes

Serving
8 Boats

INGREDIENTS

- 18 bacon slices.
- Seven large eggs.
- 1 ½ cups (170g) cheddar cheese.
- 4 tbsp thick cream.
- ½ tsp black pepper.
- ½ tsp onion powder.
- ½ tsp paprika.

INSTRUCTIONS

1. Preheat oven at 375.
2. In a large muffin tray, line each hole with bacon slices, ensuring no gaps at the bottom or on the sides. Bake for 15 minutes.
3. In a large bowl, whisk eggs, cream, black pepper, onion powder, and paprika.
4. In each bacon cup, spoon in 2 tbsp of cheese and top with egg mixture.
5. Bake for 15 minutes until eggs are completely cooked and turning golden brown.

Nutrition Per Boat: Calories: 468, Protein: 19 g, Fat: 42 g, Net Carbs: 3 g

Blueberry Breakfast Smoothie

TIME TO PREPARE
05 Minutes

COOK TIME
00 Minutes

Serving
1 People

INGREDIENTS

- ½ cup (70g) ice (crushed).
- ½ cup (120g) of thick cream or single cream.
- ½ cup (90g) blueberries.
- 3 tbsp Greek yogurt (full fat).
- 1 ½ tbsp macadamia oil.

INSTRUCTIONS

1. Put all ingredients into a blender until thick and creamy.

Nutrition Per Serving: Calories: 293, Protein: 5 g, Fat: 27 g, Net Carbs: 6 g

Tasty Turkey Rolls

TIME TO PREPARE
10 Minutes

COOK TIME
30 Minutes

Serving
1 People

INGREDIENTS

- One turkey slice.
- One large egg.
- 2 tbsp cheddar cheese (grated).
- 1 tsp mixed herbs (chopped).
- Cooking spray.

INSTRUCTIONS

1. Spray a frying pan with cooking spray and heat on medium.
2. Whisk egg and herbs together and pour into a hot frying pan.
3. Swirl the mixture around the pan until all of the pan is coated.
4. When the bottom is firm, flip the egg and add cheese.
5. When completely cooked through, remove from pan and line the turkey slice in the middle; roll into a sausage shape.

Nutrition Per Serving: Calories: 216, Protein: 18 g, Fat: 15 g, Net Carbs: 1 g

Pumpkin Pots

TIME TO PREPARE
5 Minutes

COOK TIME
10 Minutes

Serving
1 People

INGREDIENTS

- One large egg.
- 2 tbsp swerve.
- 2 tbsp flaxseed.
- 2 tbsp pumpkin puree.
- 2 tbsp almond flour.
- 1 ½ tsp pumpkin spice.
- ¼ tsp baking powder.
- Cooking spray.

INSTRUCTIONS

1. Spray a small ramekin with cooking spray and crack in egg and pumpkin puree; mix until well combined.
2. In a bowl, mix swerve, flaxseed, almond flour, pumpkin spice, and baking powder until well combined; add to egg mixture.
3. Microwave on high for 1 ½ minute until thoroughly cooked.
4. Let stand for 1 minute.

Nutrition Per Serving: Calories: 239, Protein: 13 g, Fat: 17 g, Net Carbs: 4 g

Keto Zucchini Boats

TIME TO PREPARE
10 Minutes

COOK TIME
30 Minutes

Serving
4 People

INGREDIENTS

- 3 Zucchini or courgette
- 100g (1 Cup) precut Bacon
- 50g (3Tbsp) Cream Cheese
- 100g (1cup) Blue Cheese
- 100g (1 Cup) Gouda Cheese
- 4 basil leaves cut
- salt
- pepper
- Instructio

INSTRUCTIONS

1. Preheat the oven to 190C or 370F
2. Wash and Cut Zucchinis.
3. Cut each of the zucchinis diagonally halfway through.
4. With spoon or knife, clean the inside of both of the sides.
5. Place all of the fillings as per the recipe into a big bowl and properly mix it all together.
6. Fill each half of Zucchinis fully and place them onto a baking sheet covered with Parchment Paper.
7. Place the Filled Zucchinis into the oven and bake fully for 30 minutes

Nutrition Per Serving: Calories: 166, Protein: 11 g, Fat: 13 g, Net Carbs: 2 g

Coconut Chai Smoothie

TIME TO PREPARE
5 Minutes

COOK TIME
0 Minutes

Serving
1 People

INGREDIENTS

- ⅓ cup (60g) coconut cream
- 2 tbsp. low-carb plain or vanilla protein powder
- 1 tbsp. MCT oil
- ¼ tsp. each cinnamon and ginger
- pinch cardamom and nutmeg
- dash vanilla extract
- ½ cup strong black tea, chille

INSTRUCTIONS

1. Blend all ingredients until smooth. Add water to reach the desired consistency.

Nutrition Per Serving: Calories: 473, Protein: 25 g, Fat: 38 g, Net Carbs: 4 g

Keto Chocolate Chip Cookies

TIME TO PREPARE
5 Minutes

COOK TIME
15 Minutes

Serving
10 Cookies

INGREDIENTS

- 100 g / 1 cup almond flour (to my UK readers - ground almonds work well here, just add another 2 tbsp)
- 1 medium egg
- 2 tbsp double/heavy cream
- 2 tbsp butter unsalted, VERY soft
- 3 tbsp granulated sweetener
- 1 tsp vanilla extract
- 50 g dark chocolate/chocolate chips (85% minimum or sugar free)

INSTRUCTIONS

1. Preheat the oven to 180 Celsius/356 Fahrenheit
2. Combine all ingredients apart from the chocolate with a fork. Let the dough sit for a few minutes so the flour can absorb the moisture
3. Chop your chocolate and stir into the dough
4. Form dough balls with your hand or spoon the mixture on a baking sheet lined with baking paper. Press down into the desired shape (ca ½ cm thick)
5. Bake for ca 13 minutes or until the edges are nicely browned. They are soft when straight out of the oven but firm up as they cool down.

Nutrition Per Cookies: Calories: 132, Protein: 3 g, Fat: 11 g, Net Carbs: 1 g

Egg & Goats Cheese

TIME TO PREPARE
3 Minutes

COOK TIME
5 Minutes

Serving
4 People

INGREDIENTS

- Eight large eggs.
- One tomato (chopped).
- 2 oz goat's cheese.
- 2 tbsp water.
- ¼ cup (40g) of mixed fresh herbs (chopped).
- 1 tbsp butter.
- ½ tsp salt.
- ¼ tsp black pepper.

INSTRUCTIONS

1. Whisk together eggs, salt, pepper, and water.
2. Heat butter in a large frying pan, add egg mixture, and scramble for 2-3 minutes until cooked through, blend in tomatoes and remove from heat.
3. Fold in goat's cheese and herbs.

Nutrition Per Serving: Calories: 249, Protein: 15 g, Fat: 10 g, Net Carbs: 2 g

Egg & Bacon Sandwich

TIME TO PREPARE
5 Minutes

COOK TIME
10 Minutes

Serving
2 People

INGREDIENTS

- Four bacon slices.
- Three large eggs.
- One tomato (chopped).
- One spring onion (chopped).
- ¾ cup (120g) mozzarella.
- ¾ cup (85g) cheddar cheese.
- Cooking spray.

INSTRUCTIONS

1. Preheat the oven at 400 and line a baking tray with parchment paper.
2. Mix the cheese and spread it evenly on the tray, making a circle. Bake for 5 minutes.
3. Spray a frying pan with cooking spray, fry the bacon until crispy and remove from the pan. Spray a little more cooking spray and scramble the eggs.
4. Place the bacon and eggs on one half of the cheese circle; sprinkle on tomato and onions.
5. Fold the cheese circle in half over the bacon and eggs, press down firmly, and bake for 5 minutes.

Nutrition Per Serving: Calories: 443, Protein: 35 g, Fat: 33 g, Net Carbs: 5 g

Chorizo & Egg Breakfast

TIME TO PREPARE
10 Minutes

COOK TIME
30 Minutes

Serving
6 People

INGREDIENTS

- 12 eggs.
- 6 oz cheddar cheese (grated).
- 5 oz chorizo (chopped).
- Two spring onions (chopped).
- Salt and pepper.
- Cooking spray.

INSTRUCTIONS

1. Preheat the oven at 350 and grease a large muffin tray.
2. Add the onions and chorizo to the bottom of each muffin tray hole.
3. Whisk together eggs, cheese, salt, and pepper; pour on top of the onions and chorizo.
4. Bake for 20-25 minutes until cooked through.

Nutrition Per Serving: Calories: 335, Protein: 23 g, Fat: 27 g, Net Carbs: 2 g

Anti-Inflammatory Spice Smoothie

TIME TO PREPARE
5 Minutes

COOK TIME
0 Minutes

Serving
1 People

INGREDIENTS

- One avocado
- 2 tbsp. low-carb plain or vanilla protein powder
- ½ cup (90g) blueberries
- 1 tbsp. MCT oil
- 1 tbsp. flaxseed oil
- ¼ tsp. each turmeric, ginger, and cinnamon
- water

INSTRUCTIONS

1. Blend all ingredients until smooth.

Nutrition Per Serving: Calories: 601.2, Protein: 25 g, Fat: 49.5 g, Net Carbs: 8 g

Chocolate Coconut Crunch Smoothie

TIME TO PREPARE
5 Minutes

COOK TIME
00 Minutes

Serving
1 People

INGREDIENTS

- One avocado
- 2 tbsp. low-carb chocolate protein powder

- 1 tbsp. MCT oil
- water
- 2 tbsp. chopped almonds
- 2 tbsp. unsweetened coconut flakes

INSTRUCTIONS

1. Blend the avocado, protein powder, MCT oil, and water until smooth. Stir in the almonds and coconut flakes and serve.

Nutrition Per Serving: Calories: 633.5, Protein: 31.1 g, Fat: 53.9 g, Net Carbs: 6 g

Egg on Avocado

TIME TO PREPARE
5 Minutes

COOK TIME
15 Minutes

Serving
6 People

INGREDIENTS

- One teaspoon garlic powder
- 1/2 teaspoon sea salt
- 1/4 cup (30g) Parmesan cheese
- 1/4 teaspoon black pepper
- Three medium avocados
- Six medium eggs

INSTRUCTIONS

1. Prepare muffin tins and preheat oven to 350oF.
2. To ensure that the egg would fit inside the avocado's cavity, lightly scrape off 1/3 of the meat.
3. Place avocado on a muffin tin to ensure that it faces with the top-up.
4. Evenly season each avocado with pepper, salt, and garlic powder.
5. Add one egg to each avocado cavity and garnish tops with cheese.
6. Pop in the oven and bake until the egg white is set, around 15 minutes.
7. Serve and enjoy.

Nutrition Per Serving: Calories: 261.4, Protein: 14.5 g, Fat: 20.9 g, Net Carbs: 4 g

Protein Breakfast Shake

TIME TO PREPARE
10 Minutes

COOK TIME
0 Minutes

Serving
2 People

INGREDIENTS

- 1 cup (240g) coconut milk, unsweetened
- One scoop protein powder
- 7-ounce firm tofu
- 15 drops liquid stevia
- Two tablespoon hemp hearts

INSTRUCTIONS

1. Add all ingredients into the blender and blend until you get a thick consistency.
2. Serve and enjoy.

Nutrition Per Serving: Calories: 243.5, Protein: 21 g, Fat: 13.5 g, Net Carbs: 10.1 g

Healthy Breakfast Granola

TIME TO PREPARE
5 Minutes

COOK TIME
15 Minutes

Serving
5 People

INGREDIENTS

- 1 cup (120g) walnuts, diced
- 1 cup (120g) unsweetened coconut flakes
- Two tablespoon coconut oil, melted
- Four packets Splenda
- Two teaspoon cinnamon

INSTRUCTIONS

1. Preheat the oven to 375 F/ 190 C.
2. Spray a baking tray with cooking spray and set aside.
3. Add all ingredients into the medium bowl and toss well.
4. Spread bowl mixture on a prepared baking tray and bake in preheated oven for 10 minutes.
5. Serve and enjoy.

Nutrition Per Serving: Calories: 458.2, Protein: 11.4 g, Fat: 42.7 g, Net Carbs: 11 g

Keto Coffee

TIME TO PREPARE
20 Minutes

COOK TIME
00 Minutes

Serving
2 People

INGREDIENTS

- 1 cup (10g) of black coffee (brewed)
- 1 tbsp. of butter
- 1/2 tbsp. of coconut oil
- One teaspoon of cinnamon

INSTRUCTIONS

1. Brew black coffee.
2. In a blender, combine coconut oil, coffee, and butter.
3. Blend well. Add cinnamon or stevia and serve!

Nutrition Per Serving: Calories: 260.2, Protein: 1 g, Fat: 26.2 g, Net Carbs: 0 g

Lunch recipes

Garlic Chicken with Cauliflower Mash

TIME TO PREPARE
5 Minutes

COOK TIME
50 Minutes

Serving
4 People

INGREDIENTS

Cauliflower mash:

- One large cauliflower head (chopped).
- One cup (100g) of chicken stock.
- 3 tbsp butter (cubed).
- 1 tsp salt.
- 1 tsp fresh thyme (chopped).

Garlic chicken:

- 32 oz chicken drumsticks.
- Six garlic cloves (finely chopped).
- ½ cup (40g) fresh parsley (chopped).
- 2 oz butter.
- Juice of 1 lemon.
- 2 tbsp olive oil.

INSTRUCTIONS

1. Preheat oven at 450 degrees.
2. Place the chicken in a greased ovenproof dish.
3. Drizzle olive oil and lemon juice on the chicken and top with garlic and parsley.
4. Bake for 40-45 minutes or until chicken is thoroughly cooked through and browned. Cauliflower mash:
5. In a large pan, bring chicken stock and salt to boil.
6. Add cauliflower, bring back to boil, reduce heat and simmer for 15-20 minutes, or until cauliflower is tender.
7. Take cauliflower from the pan and add to a blender with 3 tbsp of the stock.
8. Add the butter and thyme; blend until smooth and well combined.

Nutrition Per Serving: Calories: 694, Protein: 48.5 g, Fat: 49.1 g, Net Carbs: 11 g

Coconut Chicken Curry

TIME TO PREPARE
5 Minutes

COOK TIME
30 Minutes

Serving
4 People

INGREDIENTS

- 27 oz coconut milk.
- 16 oz chicken thighs (boneless and skinless, cubed).
- 8 oz broccoli (cut into small florets).
- 3 oz green beans (cut in half).
- One onion (finely chopped).
- One chili pepper (finely chopped).
- 3 tbsp coconut oil.
- 1 tbsp fresh ginger (grated).
- 1 tbsp curry paste.
- Salt and Pepper.

Cauliflower rice:

- 24 oz cauliflower head (grated).
- 3 oz coconut oil.

- ½ tsp salt.

INSTRUCTIONS

1. Heat coconut oil in a frying pan. Add onion, chili, and ginger and fry until softened.
2. Add chicken and curry paste; fry until chicken is cooked and lightly browned.
3. Add broccoli and green beans.
4. Add a substantial part of coconut milk, salt, and Pepper. Allow simmering for 15-20 minutes.
5. In another large frying pan, add 3 oz coconut oil. When hot, add the grated cauliflower.
6. Add salt and cook for 5-10 minutes until rice has softened.
7. Place rice on a serving plate and top with chicken curry.

Nutrition Per Serving: Calories: 1190, Protein: 32 g, Fat: 112 g, Net Carbs: 12 g

Egg Medley Muffins

TIME TO PREPARE
10 Minutes

COOK TIME
30 Minutes

Serving
6 People

INGREDIENTS

- 12 large eggs.
- One onion (finely chopped).
- 6 oz cheddar cheese (grated).
- 5 oz bacon (cooked and diced).
- Pinch salt and pepper.

INSTRUCTIONS

1. Preheat the oven at 175 degrees and grease a 12-hole muffin tray.
2. Equally, place onion and bacon to the bottom of each muffin tray hole.
3. In a large bowl, whisk the eggs, cheese, salt, and pepper.
4. Pour the egg mixture into each hole; on top of the onions and bacon.
5. Bake for 20-25 minutes, until browned and firm to the touch.

Nutrition Per Serving: Calories: 332, Protein: 22.5 g, Fat: 28 g, Net Carbs: 2 g

Mushroom Pork Chops

TIME TO PREPARE
5 Minutes

COOK TIME
35 Minutes

Serving
4 People

INGREDIENTS

- 4 pork chops
- salt and pepper to taste
- 1 clove garlic, crushed
- 1 onion, chopped

- 225g (8 oz) fresh mushrooms, sliced
- 1 tin condensed cream of mushroom soup

INSTRUCTIONS

1. Season pork chops with salt and pepper to taste.
2. In a large frying pan, brown the chops over medium high heat. Add the onion, garlic and mushrooms, and sauté for one minute. Pour cream of mushroom soup over chops. Cover frying pan, and reduce temperature to medium low. Simmer 20 to 30 minutes, or until chops are cooked through.

Nutrition Per Serving: Calories: 270.3, Protein: 17 g, Fat: 22.3 g, Net Carbs: 1 g

Speedy roast chicken

TIME TO PREPARE
10 Minutes

COOK TIME
60 Minutes

Serving
8 People

INGREDIENTS

- 1 whole chicken
- 1 tablespoon olive oil
- 1/4 teaspoon salt
- 1/4 teaspoon ground black pepper
- 1/4 teaspoon dried oregano
- 1/4 teaspoon dried basil
- 1/4 teaspoon paprika
- 1/8 teaspoon cayenne pepper

INSTRUCTIONS

1. Preheat oven to 230 C / Gas 8.
2. Put chicken into a small roasting tin. Rub with olive oil. Mix the spices together and rub into the chicken.
3. Roast the chicken in the preheated oven for 20 minutes. Lower the oven temperature to 200 C / Gas mark 6 and continue roasting 40 minutes, to a minimum internal temperature of 85 C. Remove from oven and let sit 10 to 15 minutes, and serve.

Nutrition Per Serving: Calories: 188.5, Protein: 15 g, Fat: 12.3 g, Net Carbs: 4 g

Tantalizing Tuna & Spinach Mix

TIME TO PREPARE
5 Minutes

COOK TIME
15 Minutes

Serving
2 People

INGREDIENTS

- Four large eggs.
- 10 oz tinned tuna (in olive oil).
- ½ cup (120g) mayonnaise.
- One avocado (sliced).
- One onion (finely diced).
- Salt and pepper (to season).

INSTRUCTIONS

1. Bring a large pan of water to a boil and lower in the eggs. Cook for 8 minutes.
2. In a bowl, mix tuna, mayonnaise, onion, salt, and pepper.
3. Chop the hard-boiled eggs into halves and place them on a plate with avocado slices and spinach.
4. Place the tuna mixture on top of spinach.

Nutrition Per Serving: Calories: 953, Protein: 53 g, Fat: 80.3 g, Net Carbs: 3.1 g

Low Carb Keto Pancakes

TIME TO PREPARE
10 Minutes

COOK TIME
35 Minutes

Serving
6 Pancakes

INGREDIENTS

- 2 large eggs
- 1 tablespoon water
- 2 oz cream cheese, cubed
- 2/3 cup almond flour
- 1 teaspoon baking powder
- 2 teaspoons vanilla extract
- 1/2 teaspoon cinnamon
- 1/2 teaspoon Sweetleaf - stevia sweetener (or 2 tablespoons regular sugar)
- butter and syrup (sugar free syrup for low carb option)

INSTRUCTIONS

1. Add all ingredients to blender. Start with eggs and water and cream cheese so you don't have anything get stuck at bottom.
2. Blend until smooth, scraping down the sides if needed. Let batter sit for 2 minutes.
3. Heat a non-stick skillet to medium heat. For each pancake, pour 3 to 4 tablespoons of batter onto skillet.
4. Once you start to see little bubbles form, flip and continue to cook until pancake is browned on each side. Continue until you have used all pancake batter.
5. Serve pancakes topped with butter and syrup!

Nutrition Per Serving (3 Pancakes): Calories: 391, Protein: 14 g, Fat: 33 g, Net Carbs: 3 g

Garlic Butter Chicken

TIME TO PREPARE
10 Minutes

COOK TIME
30 Minutes

Serving
4 People

INGREDIENTS

- Four chicken breasts (defrosted).
- 6 oz butter (room temperature).
- One garlic clove (crushed).
- 3 tbsp olive oil.
- 1 tsp lemon juice.
- ½ tsp salt.
- ½ tsp garlic powder.

INSTRUCTIONS

1. Mix butter, garlic powder, garlic clove, lemon juice, and salt. When well combined, set aside.

2. In a large frying pan, heat the oil and fry chicken breasts until completely cooked through and golden brown.
3. Place chicken on a plate and smoothly smother each chicken breast with garlic butter mixture.

Nutrition Per Serving: Calories: 899, Protein: 62 g, Fat: 72.1 g, Net Carbs: 2 g

Coconut Keto Chicken Curry

TIME TO PREPARE
5 Minutes

COOK TIME
30 Minutes

Serving
4 People

INGREDIENTS

- 24 oz chicken thighs (lean & defrosted).
- One ¼ cup (360g) coconut milk.
- ⅓ cup (50g) red onion (diced).
- 4 tsp curry paste.
- Cooking spray.

INSTRUCTIONS

1. Preheat the oven to 200 degrees.
2. Rub chicken with 2 tsp of curry paste. Set aside for 20-25 minutes.
3. Spray a large frying pan with cooking spray, fry onions and add in the remaining 2 tsp curry paste and fry 3-4 minutes.
4. Place chicken thighs in the pan with onions and sear for 3-4 minutes. Turn the chicken over, reduce heat, and pour in coconut milk. Simmer for 7-8 minutes.
5. Pour the curry mixture into a large ovenproof dish and bake for 15-20 minutes.

Nutrition Per Serving: Calories: 374, Protein: 34 g, Fat: 27.1 g, Net Carbs: 2 g

Broccoli Cheese Baked Bites

TIME TO PREPARE
10 Minutes

COOK TIME
35 Minutes

Serving
24 Bites

INGREDIENTS

- Two cups (170g) broccoli (florets).
- Two eggs.
- One cup (120g) cheddar cheese (grated).

- ½ cup (70g) spinach.
- ¼ cup (38g) onions (diced).
- ¼ cup (25g) parmesan (grated).
- ⅓ cup (60g) sour cream.
- One lemon zest.

INSTRUCTIONS

1. Preheat the oven to 180 degrees.
2. Place broccoli in a microwave-safe bowl with ¼ cup of water. Microwave for 3 minutes on high or until broccoli is tender.
3. Chop broccoli florets into small pieces and place in a large bowl. Add all other ingredients and mix well until thoroughly combined.
4. Line an ovenproof dish with greaseproof paper and pour in the mixture.
5. Bake for 25-30 minutes until puffed and browned.
6. Cool for 10 minutes and cut into 24 square bites.

Nutrition Per Serving: Calories: 61, Protein: 6 g, Fat: 6 g, Net Carbs: 1 g

Blueberry Smoothie

TIME TO PREPARE
5 Minutes

COOK TIME
0 Minutes

Serving
2 People

INGREDIENTS

- 1 large avocado
- 1/2 cup (10g) frozen blueberries
- 4 tsp flax seeds
- 2 tbsp collagen powder
- 1 1/2 cups (350 ml) of almond milk

INSTRUCTIONS

1. Put all the ingredients into a blender, and blend until smooth.

Nutrition Per Serving: Calories: 257, Protein: 10 g, Fat: 20 g, Net Carbs: 5 g

Buttered Cabbage Stir Fry

TIME TO PREPARE
5 Minutes

COOK TIME
20 Minutes

Serving
1 People

INGREDIENTS

- 5 oz cabbage (cut in long strips).
- 2 oz butter.
- Two bacon slices (diced).

INSTRUCTIONS

1. In a large frying pan, melt half of the butter and fry the bacon until crispy.
2. Add the remaining butter and stir in the cabbage; cook until cabbage begins to change color.

Nutrition Per Serving: Calories: 380, Protein: 4 g, Fat: 43 g, Net Carbs: 3 g

Golden Zucchini Chomps

TIME TO PREPARE
10 Minutes

COOK TIME
35 Minutes

Serving
2 People

INGREDIENTS

- One zucchini/courgette.
- Two garlic cloves.
- 8 oz of goat's cheese (crumbled).
- 1 ½ oz baby spinach.
- 4 tbsp olive oil.
- 2 tbsp marinara sauce (unsweetened).

INSTRUCTIONS

1. Preheat the oven to 190 degrees.
2. Slice the zucchini lengthwise in half. Using a small spoon, scrape out the seeds and put them in a small bowl.
3. Finely slice the garlic cloves and fry for 1-2 minutes until lightly browned. Stir in spinach and zucchini seeds and fry until soft.
4. Place the two zucchini halves on a baking tray and spread over the marinara sauce. Top with garlic mixture and sprinkle over the goat's cheese.

5. Bake for 25-30 minutes until zucchini is tender and cheese is golden brown.

Nutrition Per Serving: Calories: 692, Protein: 28.2 g, Fat: 64.5 g, Net Carbs: 5 g

Cheese & Tomato Salad

TIME TO PREPARE
5 Minutes

COOK TIME
0 Minutes

Serving
4 People

INGREDIENTS

- 8 oz mozzarella.
- 8 oz cherry tomatoes.
- 2 tbsp green pesto.

INSTRUCTIONS

1. Rip the mozzarella into bite-size pieces and halve the tomatoes.
2. Stir in the pesto until well combined.

Nutrition Per Serving: Calories: 216, Protein: 15.2 g, Fat: 18.5 g, Net Carbs: 3 g

Bacon & Spinach Bake

TIME TO PREPARE
5 Minutes

COOK TIME
35 Minutes

Serving
4 People

INGREDIENTS

- Eight large eggs.
- 8 oz fresh spinach.
- One cup (240g) of thick or single cream.
- 5 oz bacon (diced).
- 5 oz cheddar cheese (grated).
- 2 tbsp butter.

INSTRUCTIONS

1. Preheat the oven to 175 degrees.
2. In a large frying pan, melt the butter and fry the bacon until crispy. Add in the spinach and fry until wilted. Set aside.

3. In a large bowl, whisk together the eggs and cream.
4. Pour the egg mixture into an ovenproof dish; add bacon and spinach and top with cheese.
5. Bake for 25-30 minutes until completely set and golden brown.

Nutrition Per Serving: Calories: 660, Protein: 28.2 g, Fat: 61.5 g, Net Carbs: 4 g

Meditteranean Tomato & Pepper Tapas

TIME TO PREPARE
10 Minutes

COOK TIME
0 Minutes

Serving
4 People

INGREDIENTS

- 8 oz chorizo (sliced).
- 8 oz prosciutto.
- ½ cup mayonnaise.
- 4 oz cucumber (sliced).
- 4 oz cheddar cheese (cut into sticks).
- 2 oz red bell peppers (sliced).
- ½ tsp garlic powder.
- ½ tsp chili flakes.

INSTRUCTIONS

1. In a small bowl, mix mayonnaise, garlic, and chili flakes until well combined.
2. Place the mayonnaise dip on a serving plate; arrange the meats, cheese, peppers, and cucumber around it.

Nutrition Per Serving: Calories: 661, Protein: 29.2 g, Fat: 59.5 g, Net Carbs: 5 g

Mushrooms & Cream Cheese

TIME TO PREPARE
10 Minutes

COOK TIME
30 Minutes

Serving
4 People

INGREDIENTS

- 12 mushrooms.
- 8 oz bacon.

- 7 oz cream cheese.
- 3 tbsp fresh chives (finely diced).
- 1 tbsp butter.
- 1 tsp paprika.
- ½ tsp chili flakes.

INSTRUCTIONS

1. Preheat the oven to 200 degrees.
2. In a frying pan, cook the bacon until crispy; remove the bacon, leaving the pan's fat. Allow bacon to cool, then crumble until it resembles large breadcrumbs.
3. Remove stems from the mushrooms and finely chop. Add a little butter to the bacon fat and saute the mushroom cups.
4. In a bowl, mix cream cheese, bacon, chopped mushroom stems, chives, and paprika until well combined.
5. Divide the mixture evenly into each mushroom cup; place on a baking tray and bake for 20-25 minutes or until golden brown.
6. Sprinkle chili flakes on top.

Nutrition Per Serving: Calories: 475, Protein: 13.2 g, Fat: 47.5 g, Net Carbs: 5 g

Bacon, Cheese & Herb Balls

TIME TO PREPARE
10 Minutes

COOK TIME
25 Minutes

Serving
8 Balls

INGREDIENTS

- 5 oz cheddar cheese (grated).
- 5 oz cream cheese.
- 5 oz bacon.
- 2 oz butter.

- ½ tsp chili flakes.
- ½ tsp black pepper.
- ½ tsp Italian seasoning.

INSTRUCTIONS

1. Heat the butter in a large frying pan and fry the bacon until crispy. Reserve bacon fat and chop the bacon into small pieces.
2. In a bowl, mix cream cheese, cheddar cheese, chili flakes, pepper, Italian seasoning, and bacon fat until well combined.
3. Place the cream cheese mix in the fridge for 20 minutes.
4. When the mixture is set, roll 24 balls into shape.
5. Roll each ball in the bacon pieces before serving.

Nutrition Per Ball: Calories: 273, Protein: 9 g, Fat: 29.5 g, Net Carbs: 2 g

Smoked Salmon Lettuce Wrap

TIME TO PREPARE
10 Minutes

COOK TIME
25 Minutes

Serving
8 People

INGREDIENTS

- 8 oz cream cheese
- 7 oz smoked salmon (canned and drained).
- 2 oz iceberg lettuce leaves.

- 5 tbsp mayonnaise.
- 4 tbsp chives (finely chopped).
- ½ lemon zest.

INSTRUCTIONS

1. In a large bowl, mix everything (except lettuce leaves) together until well combined.
2. Place in the refrigerator for 15-20 minutes.
3. When chilled, scoop onto lettuce leaves and serve.

Nutrition Per Serving: Calories: 263, Protein: 10 g, Fat: 24.1 g, Net Carbs: 3 g

Green Smoothie

TIME TO PREPARE
10 Minutes

COOK TIME
30 Minutes

Serving
2 People

INGREDIENTS

- 2 cups (60 g) spinach
- 1/3 cup (46 g) raw almonds
- 2 Brazil nuts
- 1 cup (240 ml) coconut milk
- 1 Tablespoon (10 g) psyllium seeds (or psyllium husks) or chia seeds

INSTRUCTIONS

1. Place the spinach, almonds, Brazil nuts, and coconut milk into the blender first.
2. Blend until pureed.
3. Add in the rest of the ingredients (greens powder, psyllium seeds) and blend well.

Nutrition Per Serving: Calories: 381, Protein: 12 g, Fat: 36 g, Net Carbs: 5 g

Special Bacon Sandwich

TIME TO PREPARE
5 Minutes

COOK TIME
20 Minutes

Serving
1 People

INGREDIENTS

- Cooking spray.
- Two large eggs.
- 1 tbsp coconut flour.
- 1 tbsp butter (salted).
- ¼ tsp baking powder.
- One slice of cheddar cheese.
- Two slices of bacon (grilled)

INSTRUCTIONS

1. Place butter in the microwave for 30 seconds or until melted.
2. Let the butter cool slightly. Mix in 1 egg, coconut flour, baking powder; microwave for one and a half minutes.
3. Allow bread to cool and slice to make two equally thin slices.
4. Using the cooking spray, fry the remaining egg to your preference. Grill the bread until toasted and crunchy.
5. Assemble the sandwich placing a slice of toast on the bottom, cheese, bacon, fried egg, top with the remaining toast.

Nutrition Per Serving: Calories: 490, Protein: 28 g, Fat: 39 g, Net Carbs: 6 g

Pesto Egg Muffins

TIME TO PREPARE
5 Minutes

COOK TIME
30 Minutes

Serving
10 Muffins

INGREDIENTS

- 2/3 cup (100g) frozen spinach, thawed and excess water removed
- 3 tbsp pesto (45g) - you can make your own pesto
- 1/2 cup (50g) kalamata or other olives, pitted
- 1/4 cup (28g) sun-dried tomatoes, chopped
- 125 g soft goat cheese or other soft type of cheese such as feta (4.4 oz)
- 6 large eggs, free-range or organic
- sea salt and black pepper, to to taste

INSTRUCTIONS

1. Preheat the oven to 175 °C/ 350 °F (fan assisted), or 195 °C/ 380 °F (conventional). Squeeze out the excess water from the spinach, deseed and slice the olives and chop the sun-dried tomatoes. Crack the eggs into a bowl.
2. Add the pesto and season with salt and pepper to taste. Mix until well combined.
3. Divide the spinach, crumbled goat cheese, sun-dried tomatoes and olives evenly into a medium-large silicon muffin pan. (If using a regular pan, lightly grease with olive oil or ghee.)
4. Pour in the egg & pesto mixture and transfer into the oven. Bake for 20 to 25 minutes or until browned on top and cooked inside.
5. When done, remove from the oven and set aside to cool down. Store in the fridge for up to 5 days. Freeze for up to 3 months.

Nutrition Per Serving (2 Muffins): Calories: 252, Protein: 13 g, Fat: 20 g, Net Carbs: 2 g

Keto Tuna Salad

TIME TO PREPARE
5 Minutes

COOK TIME
0 Minutes

Serving
4 People

INGREDIENTS

- 10 oz. (280g) canned tuna (drained)
- 1 large avocado
- 1 celery rib
- 2 cloves fresh garlic
- 3 tablespoon mayonnaise
- 1 small red onion
- 1 tablespoon freshly squeezed lemon juice
- 1/4 cucumber
- 1 handful parsley
- 1/4 teaspoon salt
- pepper to taste

INSTRUCTIONS

1. Rinse and dry the vegetables. Finely chop the cucumber, onion, and celery. Mince the garlic.
2. Set aside half of the parsley, then add the rest of the ingredients to a large bowl.

3. Mix everything together until the avocado is well-mashed and all the ingredients have been coated. Add salt and pepper to taste.
4. Garnish with remaining parsley before serving.

Nutrition Per Serving: Calories: 225, Protein: 13 g, Fat: 16 g, Net Carbs: 3 g

Creamy Zucchini Noodles

TIME TO PREPARE
10 Minutes

COOK TIME
25 Minutes

Serving
4 People

INGREDIENTS

- 32 oz zucchini or courgette.
- 10 oz bacon (diced).
- One ¼ cups (300g) thick or single cream.
- ¼ cup mayonnaise.
- 3 oz parmesan (grated).
- 1 tbsp butter.

INSTRUCTIONS

1. Heat the cream in a large saucepan; bring to a gentle boil and allow to reduce slightly.
2. Heat the butter in a large frying pan and cook the bacon until crispy; set aside and leave grease warming in the pan (low heat).
3. Add the mayonnaise to the cream and turn down the heat.
4. Using a potato peeler, make thin zucchini strips. Cook the zucchini noodles for 30 seconds in a pan of boiling water.
5. Add cream mixture and bacon fat to the zucchini noodles; tossing to ensure all are coated. Mix in the bacon and parmesan

Nutrition Per Serving: Calories: 801, Protein: 21.2 g, Fat: 78 g, Net Carbs: 7 g

Tuna & Cheese Oven Bake

TIME TO PREPARE
10 Minutes

COOK TIME
25 Minutes

Serving
4 People

INGREDIENTS

- 16 oz tuna (tinned in olive oil).
- 5 oz celery (finely chopped).
- 4 oz parmesan (grated).
- 1 cup (230g) mayonnaise.
- One green bell pepper (diced).
- One onion (diced).
- 2 oz butter.
- 1 tsp chili flakes.

INSTRUCTIONS

1. Preheat the oven to 200 degrees.
2. In a large frying pan, fry the celery, pepper, and onion until soft.
3. In a bowl, mix tuna, mayonnaise, parmesan, and chili flakes until well combined.
4. Stir in the cooked vegetables; pour the mixture into an ovenproof dish.
5. Bake for 20-25 minutes or until golden brown.

Nutrition Per Serving: Calories: 957, Protein: 44 g, Fat: 85 g, Net Carbs: 5 g

Baked salmon

TIME TO PREPARE
5 Minutes

COOK TIME
15 Minutes

Serving
4 People

INGREDIENTS

- 4 skinless salmon fillets
- 1 tbsp olive oil or melted butter
- chopped herbs, lemon slices and steamed long-stem broccoli, to serve (optional)

INSTRUCTIONS

1. Heat the oven to 180C/160C fan/gas 4. Brush each salmon fillet with the oil or butter and season well.
2. Put the salmon fillets in an ovenproof dish. Cover if you prefer your salmon to be tender, or leave uncovered if you want the flesh to roast slightly.
3. Roast for 10-15 mins (or about 4 mins per 1cm thickness) until just opaque and easily flaked with a fork. Serve with a sprinkling of chopped herbs, lemon slices and steamed long-stem broccoli, if you like.

Nutrition Per Serving: Calories: 354, Protein: 35 g, Fat: 23 g, Net Carbs: 1 g

Herb omelette with fried tomatoes

TIME TO PREPARE
5 Minutes

COOK TIME
5 Minutes

Serving
2 People

INGREDIENTS

- 1 tsp rapeseed oil
- 3 tomatoes, halved
- 4 large eggs
- 1 tbsp chopped parsley
- 1 tbsp chopped basil

INSTRUCTIONS

1. Heat the oil in a small non-stick frying pan, then cook the tomatoes cut-side down until starting to soften and colour. Meanwhile, beat the eggs with the herbs and plenty of freshly ground black pepper in a small bowl.
2. Scoop the tomatoes from the pan and put them on two serving plates. Pour the egg mixture into the pan and stir gently with a wooden spoon so the egg that sets on the base of the pan moves to enable uncooked egg to flow into the space. Stop stirring when it's nearly cooked to allow it to set into an omelette. Cut into four and serve with the tomatoes.

Nutrition Per Serving: Calories: 205, Protein: 17 g, Fat: 13 g, Net Carbs: 3 g

Salmon & Spinach Casserole

TIME TO PREPARE
10 Minutes

COOK TIME
45 Minutes

Serving
4 People

INGREDIENTS

- 10 oz tinned salmon.
- 9 oz spinach (frozen).
- 1 ½ cups (150g) parmesan (grated).
- One cup (240g) of thick cream.
- ½ cup (120g) of almond milk.
- ¼ cup (55g) butter.
- Four slices of mozzarella.
- One garlic clove (crushed).
- 1 tbsp parsley (dried).

INSTRUCTIONS

1. Preheat the oven to 180 degrees.
2. In a large saucepan, heat the butter with the garlic. When garlic is browned, add in almond milk and cream.
3. Heat for 5-6 minutes and stir in parmesan, spinach, parsley, and salmon.
4. Constantly stir until the mixture is bubbling.
5. Pour into an ovenproof dish and top with mozzarella cheese.
6. Bake for 25-30 minutes until bubbling and golden.

Nutrition Per Serving: Calories: 640, Protein: 37 g, Fat: 54 g, Net Carbs: 5 g

Creamy chicken stew

TIME TO PREPARE
10 Minutes

COOK TIME
55 Minutes

Serving
4 People

INGREDIENTS

- 3 leeks, halved and finely sliced
- 2 tbsp olive oil, plus extra if needed
- 1 tbsp butter
- 8 small chicken thighs
- 500ml chicken stock

- 1 tbsp Dijon mustard
- 75g crème fraîche
- 200g frozen peas
- 3 tbsp dried or fresh breadcrumbs
- small bunch of parsley, finely chopped

INSTRUCTIONS

1. Tip the leeks and oil into a flameproof casserole dish on a low heat, add the butter and cook everything very gently for 10 mins or until the leeks are soft.
2. Put the chicken, skin-side down, in a large non-stick frying pan on a medium heat, cook until the skin browns, then turn and brown the other side. You shouldn't need any oil but if the skin starts to stick, add a little. Add the chicken to the leeks, leaving behind any fat in the pan.
3. Add the stock to the dish and bring to a simmer, season well, cover and cook for 30 mins on low. Stir in the mustard, crème fraîche and peas and bring to a simmer. You should have quite a bit of sauce.
4. When you're ready to serve, put the grill on. Mix the breadcrumbs and parsley, sprinkle them over the chicken and grill until browned.

Nutrition Per Serving: Calories: 400, Protein: 26 g, Fat: 27 g, Net Carbs: 6 g

Mushroom brunch

TIME TO PREPARE
5 Minutes

COOK TIME
15 Minutes

Serving
4 People

INGREDIENTS

- 250g mushrooms
- 1 garlic clove
- 1 tbsp olive oil
- 160g bag kale
- 4 eggs

INSTRUCTIONS

1. Slice the mushrooms and crush the garlic clove. Heat the olive oil in a large non-stick frying pan, then fry the garlic over a low heat for 1 min. Add the mushrooms and cook until soft. Then, add the kale. If the kale won't all fit in the pan, add half and stir until wilted, then add the rest. Once all the kale is wilted, season.
2. Now crack in the eggs and keep them cooking gently for 2-3 mins. Then, cover with the lid to for a further 2-3 mins or until the eggs are cooked to your liking. Serve with bread.

Nutrition Per Serving: Calories: 154, Protein: 13 g, Fat: 11 g, Net Carbs: 1 g

Cauliflower Soup

TIME TO PREPARE
5 Minutes

COOK TIME
20 Minutes

Serving
2 People

INGREDIENTS

- Two tablespoons olive oil
- One medium onion, finely chopped
- Three tablespoons yellow curry paste
- Two medium heads cauliflower, broken into florets
- One carton (32 ounces) vegetable broth
- 1 cup/240ml of coconut milk
- Minced fresh cilantro, optional

INSTRUCTIONS

1. In a large saucepan, heat oil over medium heat. Add onion; cook and stir until softened, 2-3 minutes.
2. Add curry paste; cook until fragrant, 1-2 minutes. Add cauliflower and broth. Increase heat to high; bring to a boil. Reduce heat to medium-low; cook, covered, about 20 minutes.
3. Stir in coconut milk; cook an additional minute. Remove from heat; cool slightly. Puree in batches in a blender or food processor.

Nutrition Per Serving: Calories: 426, Protein: 6 g, Fat: 36 g, Net Carbs: 4 g

Mexican Salmon Fillets

TIME TO PREPARE
10 Minutes

COOK TIME
20 Minutes

Serving
4 People

INGREDIENTS

- Four salmon fillets (frozen & defrosted).
- Two avocados (chopped into small cubes).
- 4 tsp Cajun seasoning.
- One jalapeno (finely diced).

- One onion (finely diced).
- 1 tbsp olive oil.
- 1 tbsp lime juice (fresh).
- 1 tbsp fresh coriander (finely diced).

INSTRUCTIONS

1. Season both sides of the salmon in Cajun seasoning.
2. Heat the oil in a frying pan; fry the salmon until browned, flip and repeat for the other side until salmon easily flakes with a fork.
3. Mix the avocados, onion, jalapenos, lime, and coriander until well combined.
4. Serve salmon and avocado mix together on a plate.

Nutrition Per Serving: Calories: 451, Protein: 33 g, Fat: 34.9 g, Net Carbs: 8 g

Salmon Buttered Cabbage

TIME TO PREPARE
5 Minutes

COOK TIME
25 Minutes

Serving
4 People

INGREDIENTS

- 16 oz salmon fillets (frozen & defrosted).
- 16 oz white cabbage.
- 4 oz butter.
- 2 oz shredded coconut (unsweetened).
- 5 tbsp olive oil.
- 1 tsp turmeric.
- ½ tsp onion powder.

INSTRUCTIONS

1. Cut the salmon into bite-size pieces and drizzle over olive oil.
2. In a small bowl, mix coconut, turmeric, and onion powder. Dip each salmon chunk into the coconut mix until the salmon is well coated.
3. In a frying pan, fry the salmon until golden brown; cover with foil and set aside.
4. Melt the butter in the frying pan and fry the cabbage until it begins to lightly brown.
5. Place the cabbage on a plate and the salmon on top; drizzle with olive oil.

Nutrition Per Serving: Calories: 768, Protein: 33 g, Fat: 70 g, Net Carbs: 3 g

Dinner recipes

Grilled Chicken Thighs Rosemary

TIME TO PREPARE
10 Minutes

COOK TIME
40 Minutes

Serving
4 People

INGREDIENTS

- 1½ lbs. (700g) chicken thighs
- Three tablespoons balsamic vinegar
- Three tablespoons extra virgin olive oil
- Three tablespoons minced garlic
- 1-½ teaspoons thyme

- Two teaspoons chopped rosemary
- ½ teaspoon pepper

INSTRUCTIONS

1. Combine balsamic vinegar with extra virgin olive oil, season with minced garlic, thyme, pepper, and chopped rosemary.
2. Rub the chicken thighs with the spice mixture, then let it rest for approximately 15 minutes.
3. In the meantime, preheat a grill over medium heat, then wait until it is ready.
4. Place the seasoned chicken thighs on the grill, then grill until all chicken sides are golden brown and cooked through. Brush the chicken thighs with the marinade once every 5 minutes.
5. Once it is done, remove the chicken from the grill and transfer to a serving dish.
6. Serve and enjoy warm.

Nutrition Per Serving: Calories: 465, Protein: 30 g, Fat: 36.2 g, Net Carbs: 2 g

Green Vegetable Soup

TIME TO PREPARE
10 Minutes

COOK TIME
20 Minutes

Serving
4 People

INGREDIENTS

- 1 bunch spring onions, chopped
- 1 large potato, peeled and chopped
- 1 garlic clove, crushed
- 1l vegetable stock
- 250g (8.4 oz.) frozen peas
- 100g (3.4 oz.) fresh spinach
- 300ml natural yogurt
- few mint leaves, basil leaves, cress or a mixture, to serve

INSTRUCTIONS

1. Put the spring onions, potato and garlic into
2. a large pan. Pour over the vegetable stock and bring to the boil.
3. Reduce the heat and simmer for 15 mins with a lid on or until the potato is soft enough to mash with the back of a spoon.
4. Add the peas and bring back up to a simmer. Scoop out around 4 tbsp of the peas and set aside for the garnish.
5. Stir the spinach and yogurt into the pan, then carefully pour the whole mixture into a blender or use a stick blender to blitz it until it's very smooth. Season to taste with black pepper.

6. Ladle into bowls, then add some of the reserved cooked peas and scatter over your favourite soft herbs or cress. Serve with crusty bread, if you like.

Nutrition Per Serving: Calories: 150, Protein: 10 g, Fat: 15 g, Net Carbs: 7 g

Marinated Chicken Lemon Jalapeno

TIME TO PREPARE
10 Minutes

COOK TIME
140 Minutes

Serving
4 People

INGREDIENTS

- 1-½ lbs. (700g) chicken thighs
- Four tablespoons extra virgin olive oil
- 2 cups (300g) chopped onion
- Two tablespoons minced garlic

- Three tablespoons chopped jalapeno
- Three tablespoons lemon juice
- Two teaspoons thyme
- 1-teaspoon cinnamon

INSTRUCTIONS

1. Combine extra virgin olive oil with lemon juice, season with onion, jalapeno, minced garlic, thyme, and cinnamon. Stir well.
2. Store in the fridge to keep it fresh.
3. After 2 hours, remove the marinated chicken from the fridge and thaw at room temperature.
4. In the meantime, preheat a grill over medium heat, then wait until it is ready.
5. Place the marinated chicken thighs on the grill until cooked through. Occasionally, brush the chicken thighs with the remaining marinade.
6. Remove the grilled chicken thighs from the grill and arrange on a serving dish.
7. Serve and enjoy.

Nutrition Per Serving: Calories: 396, Protein: 21.3 g, Fat: 31.6 g, Net Carbs: 6 g

Chicken Stew with Baby Spinach

TIME TO PREPARE
10 Minutes

COOK TIME
40 Minutes

Serving
4 People

INGREDIENTS

- 1 lb. (500g) chopped boneless chicken thighs
- Three tablespoons olive oil

- Two tablespoons garlic
- ½ teaspoon oregano
- ½ teaspoon pepper

- ½ cup (75g) halved cherry tomatoes
- 1-cup (250g) water
- ½ cup (120ml) of coconut milk
- 1 cup (30g) chopped baby spinach

INSTRUCTIONS

1. Preheat a skillet over medium heat, then pour extra virgin olive oil into it.
2. Once it is hot, stir in minced garlic, then sauté until lightly golden and aromatic.
3. Next, add chopped boneless chicken thighs to the skillet and sauté until the chicken is no longer pink.
4. Season the chicken with oregano and pepper, then pour water over the chicken. Bring to boil.
5. Once it is boiled, reduce the heat and cook until the chicken is tender and the water is completely absorbed into the chicken.
6. Pour coconut milk into the skillet and add halved cherry tomatoes to the stew. Bring to a simmer.
7. Once it is done, add chopped baby spinach to the skillet and stir well.
8. Remove the chicken stew from heat and transfer to a serving dish.
9. Serve and enjoy warm.

Nutrition Per Serving: Calories: 410, Protein: 12.3 g, Fat: 34 g, Net Carbs: 2 g

Broccoli Cheddar Soup

TIME TO PREPARE
5 Minutes

COOK TIME
20 Minutes

Serving
4 People

INGREDIENTS

- 2 tablespoons Butter
- 1/ 8 Cup (20g) White Onion
- 1/2 teaspoon Garlic, finely minced
- 2 Cups (200g) Chicken Broth
- Salt and Pepper, to taste
- 1 Cup (70g) Broccoli, chopped into bite size pieces
- 1 Tablespoon Cream Cheese
- 1/4 Cup (58g) Heavy Whipping Cream/double cream
- 1 Cup (112g) Cheddar Cheese; shredded

INSTRUCTIONS

1. In large pot, saute onion and garlic with butter over medium heat until onions are softened and translucent.
2. Add broth and broccoli to pot. Cook broccoli until tender. Add salt, pepper and desired seasoning.

3. Place cream cheese in small bowl and heat in microwave for ~30 seconds until soft and easily stirred.
4. Stir heavy whipping cream and cream cheese into soup; bring to a boil.
5. Turn off heat and quickly stir in cheddar cheese.
6. Stir in xanthan gum, if desired. Allow to thicken.

Nutrition Per Serving: Calories: 282, Protein: 12 g, Fat: 24 g, Net Carbs: 1 g

Crispy Chicken with Cheese Sauce

TIME TO PREPARE
10 Minutes

COOK TIME
40 Minutes

Serving
4 People

INGREDIENTS

- 1 lb. boneless chicken thigh
- ½ teaspoon black pepper
- 1 cup (112g) almond flour
- One egg
- ½ cup (120g) extra virgin olive oil, to fry
- 1 cup (120g) almond yogurt
- 1 cup (120g) grated cheddar cheese
- Two teaspoons mustard

INSTRUCTIONS

1. Cut the boneless chicken thigh into slices, then set aside.
2. Crack the egg, then place in a bowl.
3. Season the egg with black pepper, then stir until incorporated.
4. Dip the sliced chicken in the beaten egg, then roll in the almond flour. Make sure that the chicken is completely coated with almond flour.
5. Preheat a frying pan over medium heat, then pour olive oil into the pan.
6. Once the oil is hot, put the chicken in the frying pan and fry until both sides of the chicken are lightly golden brown and the chicken is completely cooked.
7. Place the crispy chicken on a serving dish.
8. In the meantime, place almond yogurt, grated cheddar cheese, and mustard in a saucepan, then bring to a simmer over very low heat.
9. Stir the sauce until incorporated, then remove from heat.
10. Drizzle the cheese sauce over the chicken, then serve.
11. Enjoy warm!

Nutrition Per Serving: Calories: 439.8, Protein: 12.4 g, Fat: 42.7 g, Net Carbs: 5.1 g

Sticky Chicken with Spicy Sauce

TIME TO PREPARE
15 Minutes

COOK TIME
30 Minutes

Serving
4 People

INGREDIENTS

- 1-½ lbs. boneless chicken thighs
- Two tablespoons lemon juice
- Four tablespoons extra virgin olive oil
- ½ cup (75g) chopped onion
- Two tablespoons diced green chili

- 1-tablespoon chili powder
- 1-tablespoon sweet paprika
- 1-teaspoon cumin
- ½ teaspoon oregano
- Three tablespoons tomato puree

INSTRUCTIONS

1. Preheat an oven to 250°F and line a baking tray with aluminum foil. Set aside.
2. Cut the boneless chicken thighs into slices, then rub with olive oil and lemon juice.
3. Spread chicken on the prepared baking tray, then set aside.
4. Preheat a saucepan over medium heat, then pour the remaining olive oil into it.
5. Stir in the chopped onion and sauté until aromatic and lightly golden brown.
6. After that, add tomato puree into the saucepan, season with diced green chili, chili powder, sweet paprika, cumin, and oregano. Stir well.
7. Drizzle the sauce over the chicken, then cover with aluminum foil.
8. Place the baking tray in the preheated oven and bake the chicken for approximately 30 minutes or until the chicken is cooked through.
9. Once it is done, remove the cooked chicken from the oven and rest for a few minutes.
10. Unwrap the cooked chicken and transfer to a serving dish.
11. Drizzle the remaining liquid over the chicken, then serve.

Nutrition Per Serving: Calories: 386.3, Protein: 21.5 g, Fat: 31 g, Net Carbs: 3 g

Spicy Duck with Steamed Green Collard

TIME TO PREPARE
15 Minutes

COOK TIME
45 Minutes

Serving
4 People

INGREDIENTS

- 1 ½ lbs. bone-in duck thighs
- Two tablespoons extra virgin olive oil

- Two tablespoons minced garlic
- Two teaspoons sliced shallots

- 1-teaspoon turmeric
- Three tablespoons red chili flakes
- One kaffir lime leaf
- 2 cups (500ml) of water
- ½ cup (120ml) of coconut milk
- 1 cup (235g) chopped collard green

INSTRUCTIONS

1. Preheat a steamer over medium heat, then steam the collard green until just tender.
2. Remove the steamed collard green from heat, then set aside.
3. Preheat a skillet over medium heat, then pour olive oil into it.
4. Once the oil is hot, stir in minced garlic and sliced shallots, then sauté until wilted and aromatic.
5. Next, add the duck to the skillet and season with turmeric, red chili flakes, and kaffir lime leaves.
6. After that, pour water over the duck, then bring to boil.
7. Once it is boiled, reduce the heat and cook until the duck is tender and cooked through.
8. Pour coconut milk into the skillet, then bring to a simmer. Occasionally stir the gravy until incorporated.
9. When done, remove the cooked duck, and the gravy to a serving bowl serve with steamed collard green.
10. Enjoy!

Nutrition Per Serving: Calories: 353.6, Protein: 17 g, Fat: 28.6 g, Net Carbs: 6 g

Chili Chicken Tender with Fresh Basils

TIME TO PREPARE
15 Minutes

COOK TIME
30 Minutes

Serving
4 People

INGREDIENTS

- 2 lbs. (1kg) boneless chicken thighs
- Two tablespoons minced garlic
- Two lemon kinds of grass 2 cups water
- ¼ cup (50g) diced red tomatoes
- Two tablespoons red chili flakes
- Three tablespoons extra virgin olive oil
- ½ cup (30g) fresh basils

INSTRUCTIONS

1. Cut the boneless chicken thighs into medium cubes, then place them in a skillet.
2. Season the chicken with minced garlic and lemon grasses, then pour water over the chicken. Bring to boil.
3. Once it is boiled, reduce the heat and cook until the water is completely absorbed into the chicken.
4. Remove the cooked chicken from heat, then set aside.

5. Next, preheat a saucepan over medium heat, then pour olive oil into it.
6. Stir in the chicken and cook until lightly brown.
7. Add red tomatoes, red chili flakes, and fresh basils to the saucepan, then stir until wilted and the chicken is completely seasoned.
8. Transfer the chicken to a serving dish, then serve.
9. Enjoy!

Nutrition Per Serving: Calories: 410.3, Protein: 25.6 g, Fat: 31.5 g, Net Carbs: 4 g

Chicken Avocado Creamy Salad

TIME TO PREPARE
12 Minutes

COOK TIME
30 Minutes

Serving
4 People

INGREDIENTS

- 1 lb. (500g) boneless chicken thighs
- ½ cup (120ml) almond milk
- 1-teaspoon oregano
- Two tablespoons lemon juice
- Three tablespoons extra virgin olive oil
- One ripe avocado
- Two tablespoons chopped celeries
- Two tablespoons cilantro
- ¼ cup (40g) diced onion
- ¼ teaspoon pepper

INSTRUCTIONS

1. Add oregano to the almond milk, then stir well.
2. Cut the boneless chicken thighs into slices, then rub with almond milk mixture. Let it rest for approximately 10 minutes.
3. In the meantime, preheat an oven to 250°F and line a baking tray with aluminum foil.
4. Spread the seasoned chicken on the prepared baking tray and bake until the chicken is done.
5. While waiting for the chicken, cut the avocado into halves, then remove the seed.
6. Peel the avocado, then cut into cubes.
7. Place the avocado cubes in a salad bowl, then drizzle lemon juice and extra virgin olive oil over the avocado.
8. Add chopped celeries, cilantro, onion, and pepper to the salad bowl, then toss to combine.
9. Once the chicken is done, remove from the oven and transfer to a serving dish.
10. Top the chicken with avocado salad, then serve immediately.
11. Enjoy right away.

Nutrition Per Serving: Calories: 448.2, Protein: 16.5 g, Fat: 40 g, Net Carbs: 2 g

Grilled Salmon Garlic with Tahini Sauce

TIME TO PREPARE
12 Minutes

COOK TIME
15 Minutes

Serving
4 People

INGREDIENTS

- 1 ½ lb. (700g) salmon
- One fresh lime
- Ten cloves garlic
- ¼ cup (60ml) extra virgin olive oil
- 1-teaspoon cumin
- ¾ teaspoon coriander
- 1 ½ teaspoons paprika

- ½ teaspoon black pepper
- Three tablespoons tahini paste
- ¼ cup (65ml) water
- One tablespoon lemon juice
- ¼ teaspoon garlic powder
- ¾ cup (46g) chopped parsley

INSTRUCTIONS

1. Cut the lime into halves, then squeeze the juice over the salmon. Let the salmon rest for approximately 10 minutes.
2. In the meantime, place garlic cloves in a food processor, then add extra virgin olive oil, cumin, coriander, paprika, and black pepper to the food processor. Process until smooth.
3. Wash and rinse the salmon, then pat it dry.
4. Rub the salmon with the garlic mixture, then set aside.
5. Next, prepare a grill and preheat it to medium heat.
6. Once the grill is ready, place the seasoned salmon directly on the grill and grill for approximately 5 minutes on each side.
7. Once it is done, remove the grilled salmon from the grill and transfer to a serving dish.
8. Place tahini paste and garlic powder in a food processor, then pour water and lemon juice over the paste. Process until smooth.
9. Transfer the tahini sauce to a serving bowl, then add chopped parsley to the sauce. Mix well.
10. Serve the grilled salmon with tahini sauce and enjoy warm.

Nutrition Per Serving: Calories: 298.3, Protein: 15.5 g, Fat: 24 g, Net Carbs: 5 g

Aubergine & Olive Feast

TIME TO PREPARE
5 Minutes

COOK TIME
15 Minutes

Serving
2 People

INGREDIENTS

- 10 oz halloumi (cut into slices).
- 1 aubergine (cut into bite size pieces).
- 3 oz butter.
- Twelve olives (pitted).
- 1 tsp paprika.
- 1 tsp chili flakes.

INSTRUCTIONS

1. Melt the butter in a large frying pan.
2. Place the aubergine chunks and olives in one half and halloumi in the other.
3. Season with paprika and chili; cook for 8-10 minutes, occasionally turning to ensure halloumi is golden brown on both sides and aubergine is cooked through.

Nutrition Per Serving: Calories: 849, Protein: 33 g, Fat: 77.2 g, Net Carbs: 9 g

Keto Chilli-Con-Carne

TIME TO PREPARE
10 Minutes

COOK TIME
35 Minutes

Serving
4 People

INGREDIENTS

- 16 oz minced beef (frozen & defrosted).
- 1 ½ cups (250g) canned chopped tomatoes.
- 3 oz cheddar cheese (grated).
- Two garlic cloves (crushed).
- One red onion (diced).
- ½ red pepper (diced).
- ½ yellow pepper (diced).
- 2 tsp tomato puree.
- 2 tsp coriander.
- 1 tsp chili powder.

INSTRUCTIONS

1. Preheat the oven to 180 degrees.
2. In a large frying pan, fry the onions and garlic cloves until tender. Stir in the beef and fry until browned and cooked through.

3. Add chopped tomatoes, red and yellow peppers, tomato puree, coriander, and chili powder; fry 6-7 minutes until bubbling.
4. Pour into an ovenproof dish and sprinkle cheese on top.
5. Bake for 25-30 minutes.

Nutrition Per Serving: Calories: 529, Protein: 31.2 g, Fat: 40.2 g, Net Carbs: 7 g

Almighty Almond Cheesecake

TIME TO PREPARE

10 Minutes

COOK TIME

55 Minutes

Serving

10 Cakes

INGREDIENTS

- 24 oz cream cheese.
- Four large eggs.
- 1 cup (150g) stevia.
- ⅓ cup (80g) sour cream.
- ½ tsp almond extract.

INSTRUCTIONS

1. Preheat the oven to 175 degrees.
2. In a bowl, whisk the cream cheese until smooth, then gently add stevia, sour cream, and almond extract, mix until well combined.
3. Add the eggs one by one and whisk until a thick, creamy mixture is formed.
4. Grease a springform pan, pour in the mixture, and bake for 45-50 minutes until puffed and lightly browned.
5. Remove from the oven and allow to sit at room temperature for an hour.
6. Place in the refrigerator for 5-6 hours.

Nutrition Per Cake: Calories: 529, Protein: 31.2 g, Fat: 40.2 g, Net Carbs: 7 g

Keto Blueberry Kefir Smoothie

TIME TO PREPARE

5 Minutes

COOK TIME

5 Minutes

Serving

2 People

INGREDIENTS

- 1 1/2 cup (360ml) coconut milk kefir
- 1/2 cup (75g) blueberries, fresh or frozen
- 2 tbsp MCT oil or Brain Octane Oil
- 1/2 tsp pure vanilla powder or 1-2 tsp sugar-free vanilla extract (you can make your own)
- 1/2 cup (120 ml) water + ice cubes
- Optional: 3-5 drops liquid Stevia extract or another healthy low-carb sweetener

INSTRUCTIONS

1. Place all the ingredients into a blender: kefir, blueberries, vanilla, MCT oil and ice.
2. Pulse until smooth.
3. Enjoy!

Nutrition Per Serving: Calories: 477, Protein: 4 g, Fat: 50 g, Net Carbs: 6 g

Chicken Cheese Balls with Coconut Crumbles

TIME TO PREPARE
5 Minutes

COOK TIME
25 Minutes

Serving
4 People

INGREDIENTS

- 1 lb. (500g) boneless chicken thigh
- ½ cup (60g) grated cheddar cheese
- Two eggs
- Two tablespoons almond flour
- ¼ teaspoon pepper
- 1 cup (90g) grated coconut
- ½ cup (120ml) extra virgin olive oil, to fry

INSTRUCTIONS

1. Cut the boneless chicken thigh, then Process until smooth.
2. Transfer the chicken to a mixing bowl, then add almond flour to the chicken.
3. Crack an egg and drop in the bowl and after that, mix the chicken with the almond flour and egg until combined.
4. Shape the chicken mixture into small balls, then set aside.
5. Crack the remaining egg and place it in a bowl.
6. Season the egg with pepper, then mix well.
7. Dip chicken ball in the egg mixture then rolls in the grated coconut. Make sure that the cheese balls are completely coated with grated coconut.
8. After that, preheat a frying pan over medium heat, then pour olive oil into it.

9. Once the oil is hot, carefully put the chicken cheese balls in the skillet and fry until all sides are lightly golden brown and crispy.
10. Remove the fried chicken cheese balls from the frying pan, then strain the oil.
11. Arrange the cheese balls on a serving dish and serve.
12. Enjoy immediately.

Nutrition Per Serving: Calories: 592, Protein: 125 g, Fat: 53.6 g, Net Carbs: 1.2 g

Chicken Loaf with Broccoli and Carrot

TIME TO PREPARE
10 Minutes

COOK TIME
20 Minutes

Serving
4 People

INGREDIENTS

- 1-¼ lbs. (700g) boneless chicken thighs
- Two eggs
- Three tablespoons extra virgin olive oil
- ½ cup (75g) chopped onion
- ½ teaspoon pepper
- ½ cup (80g) chopped broccoli
- ½ lb. (250g) carrots
- 1-cup cheddar cheese cubes

INSTRUCTIONS

1. Preheat a steamer and prepare a loaf pan. Coat with cooking spray and set aside.
2. Peel the carrots and cut into small dices. Set aside.
3. Cut the boneless chicken thigh into cubes, then place in a food processor. Process until smooth, then set aside.
4. Next, preheat a saucepan over medium heat, then pour olive oil into it.
5. Stir in the chopped onion and sauté until wilted and aromatic. Remove from heat.
6. Combine the chicken with eggs, then season with pepper.
7. Add sautéed onion, chopped broccoli, carrots, and cheese cubes to the chicken mixture, then mix well.
8. Transfer the chicken mixture to the prepared loaf pan, then spread evenly.
9. Place the loaf pan in the steamer and steam the chicken loaf for approximately 20 minutes.
10. Once the chicken loaf is done, remove it from the steamer and let it cool for a few minutes.
11. Take the chicken loaf out of the pan, then let it cool for about 10 minutes.
12. Cut the chicken loaf into thick slices, then arrange on a serving dish.
13. Serve and enjoy!

Nutrition Per Serving: Calories: 433.5, Protein: 24.3 g, Fat: 33 g, Net Carbs: 6.4 g

Crispy Almond Chicken with Tomato

TIME TO PREPARE
10 Minutes

COOK TIME
20 Minutes

Serving
4 People

INGREDIENTS

- ¾ lb. (375g) boneless chicken thighs
- One egg
- ¼ cup (30g) almond flour
- ½ cup (120ml) extra virgin olive oil, to fry
- 1 cup (150g) chopped onion
- ½ cup (112g) tomato puree
- ¼ teaspoon pepper

INSTRUCTIONS

1. Cut the boneless chicken thighs into thin slices, then set aside.
2. Crack the egg, then place in a bowl. Beat until incorporated.
3. Dip the sliced chicken in the beaten egg, then roll in the almond flour. Repeat with the remaining chicken and almond flour.
4. After that, preheat a pan over medium heat, then pour olive oil into it.
5. Once the oil is hot, put the coated chicken into the pan, then fry lightly golden brown, and the chicken is cooked through.
6. Discard the excessive oil.
7. Arrange the fried chicken on a serving dish, then set aside.
8. Take two tablespoons of oil, then pour into a saucepan.
9. Stir in chopped onion, then sauté until lightly golden brown and aromatic.
10. Next, add tomato puree to the saucepan, then season with pepper. Stir well and bring to a simmer.
11. Once it is done, remove the sauce from heat, then drizzle the tomato sauce over the chicken.
12. Serve and enjoy warm.

Nutrition Per Serving: Calories: 443, Protein: 17.5 g, Fat: 40.2 g, Net Carbs: 2.3 g

Zingy Lemon & Lime Pancakes

TIME TO PREPARE
10 Minutes

COOK TIME
20 Minutes

Serving
10 Pancakes

INGREDIENTS

- Four eggs.
- 2 cups (220g) almond flour.
- ¼ cup (60ml) of water.
- 8 tbsp butter (melted).
- 2 tbsp swerve.
- 1 tbsp coconut oil.
- 1 tsp baking powder.
- One lime zest
- One lemon zest

INSTRUCTIONS

1. Place all ingredients in a blender and blend until well combined.
2. Allow resting for 10-15 minutes.
3. In a frying pan, heat a little oil, pour in ⅓ cup of the butter mixture.
4. Cook for 2-3 minutes on each side until golden brown.
5. Repeat the process until all of the batters have gone.

Nutrition Per Serving: Calories: 273, Protein: 9. g, Fat: 28 g, Net Carbs: 4 g

Blueberry Whirl Mousse

TIME TO PREPARE
5 Minutes

COOK TIME
20 Minutes

Serving
8 People

INGREDIENTS

- Two cups thick whipping cream or single cream.
- 3 oz blueberries (frozen & defrosted).
- 2 oz chopped walnuts.
- ½ lemon zest.
- ¼ tsp vanilla extract.

INSTRUCTIONS

1. In a bowl, whisk the cream, vanilla, and lemon zest until soft peaks are formed.
2. Stir in the walnuts until completely combined.
3. Slightly crush the blueberries and gently swirl into the mousse.
4. Cover the bowl and place it in the refrigerator for 3-4 hours until the mousse thickens.

Nutrition Per Serving: Calories: 257, Protein: 3.1 g, Fat: 27 g, Net Carbs: 3 g

Keto Chicken Salad

TIME TO PREPARE
10 Minutes

COOK TIME
20 Minutes

Serving
2 People

INGREDIENTS

- 2 boneless chicken breasts, skin on (285 g)
- 6 thin-cut slices bacon or 3 regular slices (90 g)
- 1 large avocado, sliced (200 g)
- 4 cups (120g) mixed leafy greens of choice
- 4 tbsp Keto Ranch Dressing (60 ml/ 2 fl oz) or use dairy-free Ranch Dressing
- ghee or duck fat for greasing
- salt and pepper, to taste

INSTRUCTIONS

1. Preheat the oven to 200 °C/ 400 °F. Start by crisping up the chicken breasts. Season the chicken breasts with salt and pepper from all sides. Grease a small skillet with ghee or duck fat. Place the chicken breasts, skin side down, on the hot pan.
2. Without moving it, cook the chicken on high until golden brown and crispy, for 5-6 minutes. Then, flip the chicken on the other side, cook for 30 seconds. Transfer the skillet into the oven.
3. Cook the chicken for 10-15 minutes. It's done when an instant read thermometer inserted into the thickest part reads 74 °C/ 165 °F.
4. If you want to bake the bacon in the oven, spread the slices over a baking sheet lined with parchment paper.
5. Bake bake for 10 minutes until crispy and golden brown. Alternatively, you can crisp up the bacon separately on a frying pan.
6. Once the chicken is cooked, transfer to a cutting board and let it rest for 5 minutes.
7. Slice the avocado and the cooked chicken. Assemble the salad: start with the leafy greens, and then add avocado, crispy bacon and sliced chicken.
8. Top each salad with 2 tablespoons of Ranch Dressing.
9. This salad is best served immediately. You can always keep some cooked chicken and crisped up bacon in the fridge and reheat or simply use cold.

Nutrition Per Serving: Calories: 74, Protein: 3 g, Fat: 8 g, Net Carbs: 3 g

Pumpkin Pie Custard

TIME TO PREPARE
5 Minutes

COOK TIME
30 Minutes

Serving
4 People

INGREDIENTS

- Four large egg yolks.
- 1 ½ cups (360g) thick or single whipping cream.
- 2 tbsp erythritol.
- 2 tsp pumpkin pie spice.
- ¼ tsp vanilla extract.

INSTRUCTIONS

1. Preheat the oven to 180 degrees.
2. In a saucepan, heat cream, erythritol, pumpkin pie spice, and vanilla extract; bring to the boil.
3. Place the egg yolks into a large bowl and gradually pour in the warm cream mixture, whisking continuously.
4. Pour into an ovenproof dish and place the ovenproof dish into a larger ovenproof dish. Add water to the larger dish until it is halfway up the side of the first dish.
5. Bake for 25-30 minutes. Allow cooling before serving.

Nutrition Per Serving: Calories: 278, Protein: 5 g, Fat: 29 g, Net Carbs: 3 g

Charismatic Crepes

TIME TO PREPARE
10 Minutes

COOK TIME
25 Minutes

Serving
4 People

INGREDIENTS

- Eight large eggs.
- Two cups thick whipping cream or single cream.
- ½ cup (125ml) water (room temperature).
- 3 oz butter.
- 2 tbsp psyllium husk (powder).

INSTRUCTIONS

1. In a large bowl, whisk together eggs, cream, and water. Gradually mix in the psyllium husk until a smooth batter is formed. Allow resting for 20 minutes.
2. Use a little butter and ½ cup of batter mixture for one pancake.
3. When the top of the pancake is lightly browned and almost dry, flip and cook the other side.
4. Repeat until all batter has gone.

Nutrition Per Serving: Calories: 690, Protein: 14 g, Fat: 71 g, Net Carbs: 3.9 g

Crunchy Chocolate Coconut Curls

TIME TO PREPARE
10 Minutes

COOK TIME
25 Minutes

Serving
15 People

INGREDIENTS

- Four egg yolks.
- One cup (100g) of shredded coconut.
- One cup (160g) of dark chocolate chips (unsweetened).
- ¾ cup (90g) walnuts (chopped).
- ¼ cup (60ml) of coconut oil.
- 3 tbsp swerve.
- 3 tbsp butter.

INSTRUCTIONS

1. Preheat the oven to 175 degrees.
2. In a large bowl, mix egg yolks, coconut oil, butter, and swerve. Gradually stir in the chocolate chips, coconut, and walnuts.
3. Line a baking tray with greaseproof paper.
4. Using a tablespoon, place spoonful by a spoonful of the mixture on the tray.
5. Bake for 15-20 minutes until golden brown.

Nutrition Per Serving: Calories: 133, Protein: 3 g, Fat: 15 g, Net Carbs: 2 g

Creamiest Chocolate Dessert

TIME TO PREPARE
10 Minutes

COOK TIME
60 Minutes

Serving
2 People

INGREDIENTS

- Two avocados (ripe).
- ¾ cup (180g) of thick or single cream.
- ½ cup (80g) of chocolate chips (unsweetened).
- ¼ cup (30g) swerve.
- 3 tbsp cocoa powder (unsweetened).
- 1 tsp vanilla extract.

INSTRUCTIONS

1. Mix all ingredients in a blender until smooth.
2. Transfer mixture into two serving bowls/glasses and refrigerate for 45-60 minutes.

Nutrition Per Serving: Calories: 673, Protein: 15 g, Fat: 82 g, Net Carbs: 8 g

Tantalizing Chocolate Truffles

TIME TO PREPARE
5 Minutes

COOK TIME
25 Minutes

Serving
15 Truffles

INGREDIENTS

- One avocado (mashed).
- One cup (160g) of chocolate chips (unsweetened & melted).
- ¼ cup (25g) of cocoa powder.
- 1 tsp vanilla extract.

INSTRUCTIONS

1. In a bowl, mix avocado, chocolate, and vanilla extract until well combined and smooth.
2. Place in the refrigerator for 20-25 minutes until slightly firm.
3. Using a teaspoon, scoop out one chocolate truffle. Roll in the palm of your hand to mold it to a round shape.
4. Roll in cocoa powder and repeat until all chocolate mixture has gone.

Nutrition Per Truffle: Calories: 21, Protein: 3 g, Fat: 3 g, Net Carbs: 2 g

Perk You Up Porridge

TIME TO PREPARE
5 Minutes

COOK TIME
10 Minutes

Serving
1 People

INGREDIENTS

- 2 tbsp almond flour.
- 2 tbsp sesame seeds (ground).
- 2 tbsp flaxseed (ground).
- ½ cup (120ml) of almond milk (unsweetened).

INSTRUCTIONS

1. Mix almond flour, sesame seeds, and flax seeds in a bowl.
2. Stir in the almond milk and microwave for one minute.
3. Stir again and microwave for an additional minute.

Nutrition Per Serving: Calories: 216, Protein: 8 g, Fat: 17 g, Net Carbs: 9 g

Keto-Buzz Blueberry Pancakes

TIME TO PREPARE
10 Minutes

COOK TIME
10 Minutes

Serving
3 People

INGREDIENTS

- Three large eggs.
- ½ cup (60g) almond flour.
- ¼ cup (60ml) of milk.
- ¼ cup (50g) of fresh blueberries.
- 2 tbsp coconut flour.
- 2 tbsp sweetener (granulated).
- 1 tsp cinnamon (ground).
- ½ tsp baking powder.

INSTRUCTIONS

1. Add all ingredients (except blueberries) to a blender and mix until a thick batter is formed.
2. Add the blended mixture to a bowl and stir in blueberries.
3. Grease a large non-stick frying pan and allow the pan to get hot over medium heat.

4. Pour ¼ cup of the mixture into the hot pan, allow to cook for 2 - 3 minutes or until the edges start to crisp and turn lightly browned. Flip and repeat.
5. Repeat the process using the remaining batter.

Nutrition Per Serving: Calories: 132, Protein: 7 g, Fat: 7 g, Net Carbs: 4 g

Mozzarella Pockets of Pleasure

TIME TO PREPARE
10 Minutes

COOK TIME
30 Minutes

Serving
8 Pieces

INGREDIENTS

- Three eggs.
- 8 oz mozzarella (grated).
- 4 oz bacon (grilled).
- 2 oz cream cheese.
- ⅔ cup (75g) almond flour.

- ½ cup (60g) cheddar cheese (grated).
- ⅓ cup (38g) coconut flour.
- 2 tsp baking powder.
- 1 tsp salt.

INSTRUCTIONS

1. Preheat oven at 350 degrees.
2. Microwave the cream cheese and mozzarella for 60 seconds. Stir and microwave for an additional 60 seconds.
3. Put one egg, almond flour, coconut flour, baking powder, and salt into a blender and pour in the melted cheese mixture. Blend until a dough form.
4. Split the dough into eight pieces. Flatten each piece to form a 5-inch circle, place on a baking tray lined with baking paper.
5. Scramble the remaining two eggs and divide between each circle; do the same with bacon and cheddar cheese.
6. Fold the edges in and seal the semi-circle using fingertips.
7. Bake for 20 minutes or until lightly browned.

Nutrition Per Piece: Calories: 258, Protein: 16 g, Fat: 18 g, Net Carbs: 6 g

Strawberries smoothie

TIME TO PREPARE
15 Minutes

COOK TIME
0 Minutes

Serving
4 People

INGREDIENTS

- 8 oz strawberries (frozen & defrosted).
- 8 oz blueberries (frozen & defrosted).
- One cup () of Greek yoghurt (full fat).
- ½ cup thick or single whipping cream.
- 1 tsp orange extract.

INSTRUCTIONS

1. Place all ingredients into a blender and mix until thoroughly combined.
2. Pour into a bowl and freeze for 40-60 minutes.

Nutrition Per Serving: Calories: 74, Protein: 3 g, Fat: 8 g, Net Carbs: 4 g

Stir Fry Crab in Creamy Chili

TIME TO PREPARE
12 Minutes

COOK TIME
22 Minutes

Serving
4 People

INGREDIENTS

- Four whole crabs
- Four tablespoons minced garlic
- ¼ cup (60ml) olive oil
- ½ cup (75g) onion
- Two teaspoons green chili

- ¾ cup (180ml) of coconut milk
- Two kaffir lime leaves
- 1-cup fresh basil
- Two tablespoons lemon juice

INSTRUCTIONS

1. Cut the crabs into halves, then set aside.
2. Preheat a skillet over medium heat, then pour extra virgin olive oil into the skillet.
3. Once the oil is hot, stir in minced garlic, then sauté until wilted and aromatic.
4. Add halved crabs to the skillet, then stir until cooked and crispy.
5. Remove the crabs from heat, then place them on a plate.

6. Stir in the chopped onion and green chili to the skillet, then sauté with the remaining olive oil.
7. Pour coconut milk over the onion, then season with kaffir lime leaves. Bring to a simmer.
8. Add fresh basils to the skillet, then return the crabs to the skillet. Cook for approximately 2 minutes.
9. Once it is done, remove it from heat, then drizzle lemon juice over the crabs.
10. Transfer the crabs to a serving dish, then enjoy.

Nutrition Per Serving: Calories: 320.5, Protein: 2.5 g, Fat: 25 g, Net Carbs: 6 g

Crispy Prawn with Almond Cheesy Sauce

TIME TO PREPARE	COOK TIME	Serving
12 Minutes	20 Minutes	4 People

INGREDIENTS

- ½ lb. (250g) fresh prawns
- One egg
- ½ teaspoon pepper
- 1 cup (112g) almond flour
- ¼ cup (60ml) extra virgin olive oil, to fry
- ¼ cup (37.5g) chopped onion
- ¼ cup (60ml) water
- ½ cup (60g) grated cheese

INSTRUCTIONS

1. Peel the prawns and remove the head.
2. Crack the egg, then place in a bowl.
3. Season the egg with pepper, then stir until incorporated.
4. Dip the prawns in the egg, then roll into the almond flour. Set aside.
5. Preheat a frying pan over medium heat, then pour extra virgin olive oil into it.
6. Put the prawns in the frying pan and fry until the prawns are lightly golden brown.
7. Remove the fried prawns from the frying pan and strain the excessive oil. Arrange on a serving dish.
8. Take about two tablespoons of extra virgin olive oil, then pour into a saucepan. Preheat it over medium heat.
9. When the oil is hot, stir in the chopped onion and sauté until wilted and aromatic.
10. Pour water into the saucepan, then add grated cheese to the saucepan.
11. Stir in almond flour and stir until thick.
12. Drizzle the cheese sauce over the fried prawns' then serve.
13. Enjoy!

Nutrition Per Serving: Calories: 291.5, Protein: 5 g, Fat: 22 g, Net Carbs: 2 g

Bonus Recipes

Pure Perfection Pepperoni Pizza

TIME TO PREPARE
5 Minutes

COOK TIME
40 Minutes

Serving
2 People

INGREDIENTS

- Four large eggs.
- 6 oz mozzarella (grated)

    Topping:
- 3 tbsp tomato puree.
- 5 oz mozzarella (grated).
- 1 ½ oz pepperoni (sliced).
- ½ tsp dried mixed herbs.

INSTRUCTIONS

1. Preheat oven at 400 degrees.
2. Mix the eggs with 6oz grated mozzarella until well combined.
3. Line a baking tray with greaseproof paper. Using a spatula, spread the mixture into one large rectangular pizza.
4. Bake for 15-20 minutes until lightly browned. Remove from oven.
5. Adjust oven temperature to 450 degrees.
6. Spread tomato puree on to the pizza and sprinkle on the herbs. Load with the remaining cheese and place pepperoni on top.
7. Bake for an additional 10 minutes or until golden brown and cheese has melted.

Nutrition Per Serving: Calories: 1043, Protein: 52 g, Fat: 90 g, Net Carbs: 5

Green Chili Squid Black Pepper

TIME TO PREPARE
5 Minutes

COOK TIME
18 Minutes

Serving
4 People

INGREDIENTS

- ½ lb. (250g) fresh squids

- Three tablespoons extra virgin olive oil
- Two teaspoons minced garlic
- Two teaspoons sliced shallots
- ¼ cup (60g) chopped green chili
- ½ cup (120ml) of coconut milk
- 1-teaspoon coconut aminos
- 1-teaspoon black pepper

INSTRUCTIONS

1. Remove the squid ink and cut the squids into rings.
2. Preheat a skillet over medium heat, then pour extra virgin olive oil into the skillet.
3. Once the oil is hot, stir in minced garlic and sliced shallots, then sauté until wilted and aromatic.
4. Next, add the squid to the skillet and sauté until just wilted.
5. Pour coconut milk over the squids, then cook until the liquid is completely absorbed into the squids.
6. Add chopped green chili, coconut aminos, and black pepper to the skillet, then stir until the squids are completely seasoned and cooked through.
7. Remove the squids from heat and transfer to a serving dish.
8. Serve and enjoy.

Nutrition Per Serving: Calories: 235, Protein: 11 g, Fat: 18 g, Net Carbs: 5 g

Pan-Seared Salmon with Mushroom and Spinach

TIME TO PREPARE
5 Minutes

COOK TIME
20 Minutes

Serving
4 People

INGREDIENTS

- 1 lb. (500g) salmon fillet
- Three tablespoons extra virgin olive oil
- 1 cup (75g) chopped mushroom
- 2 cups (80g) chopped spinach
- ¼ cup (62g) chopped tomatoes
- ½ teaspoon pepper
- 1-tablespoon balsamic vinegar

INSTRUCTIONS

1. Sprinkle pepper over the salmon fillet, then set aside.
2. Preheat a pan over medium heat, then pour olive oil into it.
3. Once it is hot, put the salmon in the pan, sear it for approximately 4 minutes, and then flip it.

4. Sear the other side of the salmon and cook until it is completely done and both sides of the salmon are cooked.
5. Remove the cooked salmon from the pan and place on a plate.
6. Next, stir in mushroom, then sauté with the remaining olive oil.
7. Once the mushroom is wilted, stir in chopped spinach and tomatoes, then toss with balsamic vinegar.
8. Transfer the vegetables to a serving dish, then put the cooked salmon on top.
9. Serve and enjoy.

Nutrition Per Serving: Calories: 275, Protein: 19 g, Fat: 21.5 g, Net Carbs: 0.9 g

Intense Cauliflower Cheese Bake

TIME TO PREPARE
10 Minutes

COOK TIME
40 Minutes

Serving
6 People

INGREDIENTS

- One large cauliflower head.
- 8 oz thick cream.
- 4 oz cheddar (grated).
- 4 oz mozzarella (grated).

- 3 oz cream cheese (softened).
- 1 ½ tsp paprika.
- 1 tsp salt.
- ½ tsp black pepper.

INSTRUCTIONS

1. Preheat oven at 375 degrees.
2. Cut cauliflower into 1-inch pieces and steam for 5 minutes until just becoming tender.
3. In a medium-sized pan, combine thick cream, cheddar, mozzarella, cream cheese, salt, pepper, and paprika. Over medium heat, stirring continuously, until a smooth sauce is formed.
4. Add the cauliflower to a baking dish and pour over the cheese sauce; stir to ensure all cauliflower is covered.
5. Bake for 30 minutes or until the top is bubbling and golden.

Nutrition Per Serving: Calories: 393, Protein: 15.3 g, Fat: 33.5 g, Net Carbs: 10.5 g

Tasty Salted Turnip Fries

TIME TO PREPARE
5 Minutes

COOK TIME
40 Minutes

Serving
4 People

INGREDIENTS

- 16 oz turnips.
- 6 tbsp olive oil.
- 2 tsp onion powder.
- ½ tsp paprika.
- 1 tsp salt.

INSTRUCTIONS

1. Preheat oven at 400 degrees.
2. Wash and peel the turnips; cut into ½ inch strips.
3. In a large bowl, toss the turnips in 2 tbsp of olive oil, salt, onion powder, and paprika.
4. Add remaining oil to a baking tray and heat in the oven for 5 minutes.
5. Bake for 25-30 minutes or until fries is golden brown and crispy.

Nutrition Per Serving: Calories: 219, Protein: 2 g, Fat: 22.2 g, Net Carbs: 7 g

Chicken & pistachio salad

TIME TO PREPARE
10 Minutes

COOK TIME
10 Minutes

Serving
2 People

INGREDIENTS

- 2 large eggs
- 2 tbsp extra virgin olive oil
- 1 large lemon, zested and juiced
- 2 tbsp natural yogurt
- 1 large skinless cooked chicken breast fillet

- 40g mixed olives, halved
- 40g sundried tomatoes
- small bunch basil, chopped
- 3 Little Gem lettuces, leaves separated
- 30g pistachios, roughly chopped and toasted

INSTRUCTIONS

1. Bring a large pan of water to a simmer. Add the eggs and cook gently for 7 mins. Remove with a slotted spoon and transfer to a bowl of cold water. Once cooled, carefully peel off the shell and slice each egg in half.
2. Meanwhile, whisk the oil with the lemon zest, juice and yogurt, and season well. Shred the chicken and toss with the olives, sundried tomatoes, basil and lettuce. Pour in the dressing, season and toss together.
3. Divide the salad between two bowls and top with the egg halves and pistachios.

Nutrition Per Serving: Calories: 521, Protein: 37 g, Fat: 30 g, Net Carbs: 8 g

Healthy Lunchtime Ham & Cheese Wrap

TIME TO PREPARE
10 Minutes

COOK TIME
20 Minutes

Serving
12 People

INGREDIENTS

- Five iceberg lettuce leaves.
- Four slices sandwich ham.
- 4 slices cheddar cheese.
- ¼ cup (56g) guacamole.
- One tomato (sliced).
- ½ red onion (finely sliced)

INSTRUCTIONS

1. Layer lettuce leaves onto a sheet of cling film. Ensure the leaves overlap each other.
2. Layer the ham and cheese onto the leaves.
3. Do the same with tomato and onion and finally top with guacamole.
4. Using the clingfilm (as if you were using a sushi mat), roll the lettuce tightly to make the wrap.
5. When completely rolled, cut the wrap in half.

Nutrition Per Serving: Calories: 459, Protein: 33 g, Fat: 31.5 g, Net Carbs: 12 g

Crusted Pancetta & Onion Quiche

TIME TO PREPARE
10 Minutes

COOK TIME
60 Minutes

Serving
4 People

INGREDIENTS

Crust:
- 1 ½ cups (160g) almond flour.
- 2 oz butter.
- One large egg.
- 2 tbsp sesame seed.
- 1 tbsp psyllium husk powder.
- ½ tsp salt.

Filling:
- Five large eggs.
- 11 oz pancetta (chopped).
- 8 oz cheddar cheese (grated).
- One onion.
- One cup (240g) of thick or single cream.
- 1 oz butter.
- 1 tsp thyme (dried).
- ½ tsp salt.
- ½ tsp black pepper.

INSTRUCTIONS

1. Preheat oven at 350 degrees.
2. Take all of the crust ingredients and put them in a blender. Mix until a dough is formed.
3. Using a spatula, spread the dough into a springform cake tin. Allow settling in the fridge.
4. Melt the butter in a large frying pan, add the onion and pancetta and fry until both turn golden brown. Stir in thyme, salt, and pepper.
5. Pour into set crust.
6. In a bowl, mix the remaining ingredients and pour into crust.
7. Bake for 45-50 minutes or until the egg mixture is solid and has turned golden brown.

Nutrition Per Serving: Calories: 885, Protein: 26 g, Fat: 82.5 g, Net Carbs: 5 g

Spicy Tuna No-Rice Sushi Rolls

TIME TO PREPARE
20 Minutes

COOK TIME
0 Minutes

Serving
2 People

INGREDIENTS

- One cucumber.
- ½ can tuna (in olive oil).

- ½ avocado (sliced).
- 1 tsp chili sauce.
- ¼ tsp salt.
- ¼ tsp black pepper.
- Pinch of cayenne pepper

INSTRUCTIONS

1. Using a potato peeler, thinly slice cucumber (lengthways) until the outer layer has gone. Discard the outer layer and thinly slice the cucumber until you have six long strips.
2. In a medium bowl, mix tuna, chili sauce, salt, pepper, and cayenne until well combined.
3. Take a cucumber slice and spoon the mixture over, leaving half an inch at each end.
4. Place 1-2 pieces of avocado on each cucumber slice and carefully roll.
5. Use a toothpick to secure.

Nutrition Per Serving: Calories: 123, Protein: 10 g, Fat: 9.5 g, Net Carbs: 2 g

Mighty Meaty Moussaka

TIME TO PREPARE
15 Minutes

COOK TIME
40 Minutes

Serving
4 People

INGREDIENTS

- 20 oz minced beef.
- One medium aubergine (thinly sliced).
- One onion (finely chopped).
- Two garlic cloves (crushed).
- ½ cup (112g) tomato puree.
- 4 tbsp olive oil.
- 1 tbsp paprika powder.
- 1 tsp salt.

- ½ tsp black pepper.
- ½ tsp cinnamon (ground).

Cheese sauce:
- 7 oz swiss cheese (grated).
- 3 oz cream cheese.
- ½ cup (120g) thick or single cream
- One garlic clove (crushed).
- ¼ tsp salt.

INSTRUCTIONS

1. Preheat oven at 350 degrees.
2. In a large frying pan, fry the aubergine slices until golden brown and softened. Set to one side.
3. In the same pan, cook the minced beef until browned. Add onion, garlic, and spices; pour in the tomato puree and simmer for 5 minutes.
4. In a pan, mix the cheese sauce ingredients (only using half of the swiss cheese). Stirring continuously, Simmer until sauce thickens.
5. Pour meat sauce into an ovenproof dish, layer the auberges on top and pour on the cheese sauce. Sprinkle the remaining swiss cheese on top.

6. Bake for 20-25 minutes or until cheese turns golden brown.

Nutrition Per Serving: Calories: 772, Protein: 43 g, Fat: 59 g, Net Carbs: 12 g

Keto Chili Kicker

TIME TO PREPARE
10 Minutes

COOK TIME
20 Minutes

Serving
4 People

INGREDIENTS

- 16 oz minced beef
- Two avocados (chopped).
- One tomato (finely chopped).
- One garlic clove (crushed).
- 3 tbsp lime juice (fresh).
- 2 tbsp red onion (finely chopped).

- 1 tbsp coriander (ground).
- 1 tbsp cumin (ground).
- ½ tsp cayenne pepper.
- ½ tsp garlic powder.
- ¼ tsp black pepper.

INSTRUCTIONS

1. In a large frying pan, add minced beef, coriander, cumin, cayenne pepper, and garlic powder. Fry for 6-8 minutes or until beef is completely cooked.
2. In a bowl, mix avocados, tomatoes, crushed garlic, onion, lime juice, and black pepper; mix until well combined.
3. Put chili into a bowl and serve avocado salsa on top.

Nutrition Per Serving: Calories: 313, Protein: 35 g, Fat: 15 g, Net Carbs: 5 g

Spicy Infused Shrimp

TIME TO PREPARE
10 Minutes

COOK TIME
50 Minutes

Serving
4 People

INGREDIENTS

- 32 oz jumbo shrimp (peeled and deveined).
- Four garlic cloves (chopped).
- 1 cup basil leaves.

- ¼ cup parmesan (grated).
- ¼ cup (30g) walnuts (chopped).
- 6 tbsp olive oil.
- ½ tsp salt.

- ¼ tsp chili flakes.

INSTRUCTIONS

1. In a blender, add olive oil, basil, garlic, chili, salt, parmesan, and walnuts. Blend until well combined.
2. Set 2 tbsp of pesto aside
3. Add shrimp to the large bowl of pesto and ensure all shrimp are covered. Let marinate for 30-40 minutes.
4. Using cooking spray, spray a wire rack, so it is thoroughly coated.
5. Place shrimp on wire rack and grill for 5 minutes on each side or until slightly charred.
6. Serve the shrimp, using the remaining pesto to taste.

Nutrition Per Serving: Calories: 259, Protein: 24 g, Fat: 17 g, Net Carbs: 3 g

Gorgeous Garlic Gnocchi

TIME TO PREPARE
10 Minutes

COOK TIME
50 Minutes

Serving
4 People

INGREDIENTS

- One ⅓ cup (150g) almond flour.
- ⅔ cup (67g) parmesan (grated).
- ½ cup (125g) ricotta cheese.
- One large egg.
- Four garlic cloves (chopped).
- 2 tbsp coconut flour.

- 2 tbsp butter.
- 2 tbsp olive oil.
- 2 tsp xanthan gum.
- 1 tsp garlic powder.
- ¼ tsp salt.

INSTRUCTIONS

1. In a bowl, mix almond flour, coconut flour, garlic powder, and xanthan gum.
2. In a separate bowl, whisk the egg and add ricotta, parmesan, and salt; mix until well combined.
3. Add the flour mixture to the cheese mixture and mix thoroughly until the crumble becomes a sticky dough ball.
4. Wrap the dough ball in cling film and let settle in the fridge for 60 minutes.
5. Cut the dough into 1-inch pieces, molding them into an oval shape.
6. In a large frying pan, add olive oil and butter; fry the garlic until lightly browned.
7. Fry the gnocchi for 5 minutes, spooning on the garlic oil.

Nutrition Per Serving: Calories: 314, Protein: 13 g, Fat: 27.5 g, Net Carbs: 7 g

Bacon & avocado frittata

TIME TO PREPARE
10 Minutes

COOK TIME
25 Minutes

Serving
4 People

INGREDIENTS

- 8 rashers smoked streaky bacon
- 3 tbsp olive oil
- 6 eggs, beaten
- 1 large avocado, halved, stoned, peeled and cut into chunky slices
- 1 small red chilli, finely chopped

- 1 heaped tsp Dijon mustard
- 2 tsp red wine vinegar
- 200g bag mixed salad leaves (we used watercress, rocket & spinach)
- 12 baby plum tomatoes, halved

INSTRUCTIONS

1. Heat a 24cm non-stick ovenproof pan and fry the bacon rashers in batches on a high heat until cooked through and crisp. Chop 4 roughly and break the other 4 into large pieces. Set aside on kitchen paper and clean the pan.
2. Heat the grill to high. Warm 1 tbsp oil in the pan. Season the eggs, add the chopped bacon and pour into the pan. Cook on a low heat for around 8 mins or until almost set. Arrange the avocado slices and bacon shards on top. Grill briefly for about 4 mins until set.
3. Mix the remaining oil, the chilli, mustard, vinegar and seasoning in a large bowl. Toss in the salad leaves and tomatoes. Serve alongside the frittata, cut into wedges.

Nutrition Per Serving: Calories: 467, Protein: 22 g, Fat: 38.2 g, Net Carbs: 2 g

Charming Keto Carrot Cake

TIME TO PREPARE
10 Minutes

COOK TIME
10 Minutes

Serving
2 People

INGREDIENTS

- ¾ cup (84g) almond flour.
- ½ cup (30g) carrot (grated)
- One large egg.
- 2 tbsp cream cheese.
- 2 tbsp walnuts (finely chopped).
- 2 tbsp butter (melted).

- 2 tbsp erythritol.
- 1 tbsp thick cream.
- 2 tsp cinnamon.
- 1 tsp mixed spice.
- 1 tsp baking powder.

INSTRUCTIONS

1. In a bowl, mix almond flour, cinnamon, baking powder, erythritol, walnuts, and mixed spice.
2. Mix in the egg, butter, thick cream, and carrot until well combined.
3. Grease 2 microwave-safe ramekins and split the mixture evenly between the two.
4. Microwave on high for 5 minutes.
5. Spread cream cheese on the top.

Nutrition Per Serving: Calories: 443, Protein: 14 g, Fat: 40.5 g, Net Carbs: 5 g

Indulgence Peanut Butter Biscuits

TIME TO PREPARE
10 Minutes

COOK TIME
25 Minutes

Serving
8 Biscuits

INGREDIENTS

- 1 cup (112g) almond flour.
- ½ cup (125g) of peanut butter (unsweetened).
- ⅓ cup (40g) erythritol.
- 1 tbsp coconut oil.
- ¾ tsp baking powder.
- ½ tsp vanilla extract.

INSTRUCTIONS

1. Preheat oven at 350 degrees.
2. In a large bowl, mix all of the ingredients until a dough is formed.
3. Divide the dough into eight large biscuits.
4. Line a baking tray with greaseproof paper.
5. Bake for 10-12 minutes or until golden brown.

Nutrition Per Biscuit: Calories: 189.5, Protein: 7 g, Fat: 16 g, Net Carbs: 5.9 g

Chewy Coconut Chunks

TIME TO PREPARE
10 Minutes

COOK TIME
40 Minutes

Serving
16 Chunks

INGREDIENTS

- 7 oz coconut (shredded).
- ⅔ cup (160g) of coconut milk (full fat).
- ¼ cup (25g) erythritol.
- 1 tsp psyllium husk.
- ¼ tsp almond extract.
- ¼ tsp salt.

INSTRUCTIONS

1. Preheat oven at 325 degrees.
2. In a blender, mix coconut milk, maple syrup, psyllium husk, almond extract, salt, and ¾ of the coconut flakes until smooth.
3. Pour mixture into a large bowl, stir in remaining coconut flakes.
4. Line a baking tray with greaseproof paper. Using a tablespoon, scoop out chunks of the mixture and place onto the tray.
5. Bake for 30 minutes or until all chunks are golden brown.

Nutrition Per Chunk: Calories: 112, Protein: 2 g, Fat: 10 g, Net Carbs: 6.5 g

Lamb & lettuce pan-fry

TIME TO PREPARE
7 Minutes

COOK TIME
15 Minutes

Serving
4 People

INGREDIENTS

- 25g butter
- 4 lamb neck fillets, cut into chunks
- 2 handfuls frozen peas
- 150ml chicken stock
- 3 Baby Gem lettuces, cut into quarters

INSTRUCTIONS

1. Heat the butter in a frying pan until sizzling, then add the lamb. Season with salt, if you like, and pepper, then cook for 6-7 mins until browned on all sides. Scatter in the peas, pour in the stock, then bring up to a simmer and gently cook until the peas have defrosted.
2. Add the lettuce to the pan and simmer for a few mins until just starting to wilt, but still vibrant green. Serve!

Nutrition Per Serving: Calories: 465, Protein: 30 g, Fat: 37 g, Net Carbs: 2 g

Spicy Crispy Squids with Onion

TIME TO PREPARE
5 Minutes

COOK TIME
15 Minutes

Serving
4 People

INGREDIENTS

- ½ lb. (250g) fresh squids
- One big onion
- 1-cup (112g) almond flour
- ½ teaspoon pepper
- One egg

- ¾ cup (187.5ml) of water
- ½ cup (125ml) olive oil
- ¼ cup (35g) chopped red chili
- Two teaspoon garlic

INSTRUCTIONS

1. Cut the squids and onion into rings, then set aside.
2. Place almond flour in a bowl, then season with pepper.
3. Crack the egg and add to the almond flour, then pour water over the almond flour. Stir until incorporated. Set aside.
4. Preheat a frying pan over medium heat, then pour olive oil into it.
5. Dip the onion ring in the almond flour mixture, then fry.
6. Once the onion is done, do the same thing to the squids.
7. Next, take about two tablespoons of olive oil, then pour into a pan.
8. Stir in minced garlic and chopped red chili, then sauté until wilted and aromatic.
9. Add fried onion and squid rings to the pan, then stir until the rings are completely seasoned.
10. Remove from heat and transfer then crispy squids to a serving dish.
11. Serve and enjoy warm.

Nutrition Per Serving: Calories: 358, Protein: 14 g, Fat: 4 g, Net Carbs: 6 g

Garden salmon salad

TIME TO PREPARE
8 Minutes

COOK TIME
45 Minutes

Serving
4 People

INGREDIENTS

- 2 courgettes
- 100g fresh shelled peas
- 8 radishes, halved
- 3 tbsp rapeseed oil
- 1 large lemon, zested and juiced
- 2 tbsp fat-free natural yogurt

- 75g pea shoots
- 4 poached salmon fillets, skin removed and flaked into large chunks
- 2 tbsp mixed seeds
- 1/2 small bunch dill, fronds picked

INSTRUCTIONS

1. Cut the courgettes into long thin strips using a peeler, and discard the soft, seeded core. Toss the courgette ribbons, peas and radishes together in a large bowl. Whisk the oil, lemon zest and juice, and yogurt together, then toss with the veg.
2. Put the pea shoots, dressed veg and large flakes of salmon on a large platter. Finish with a good grinding of black pepper, and scatter over the mixed seeds and dill to serve.

Nutrition Per Serving: Calories: 315, Protein: 16 g, Fat: 26 g, Net Carbs: 3 g

Surprise Recipes

Creamy Tuscan Garlic Chicken

TIME TO PREPARE
10 Minutes

COOK TIME
15 Minutes

Serving
2 People

INGREDIENTS

- 1 pounds boneless skinless chicken breasts thinly sliced
- 2 Tablespoons olive oil
- 1 cup (240g) heavy or single cream
- 1/2 cup (50g) chicken broth

- One teaspoon garlic powder
- One teaspoon Italian seasoning
- 1/2 cup (50g) parmesan cheese
- 1 cup (30g) spinach chopped
- 1/2 cup (27g) sun-dried tomatoes

INSTRUCTIONS

1. In a large skillet, add olive oil and cook the chicken on medium-high heat for 3-5 minutes on each side or until brown on each side and cooked until no longer pink in center. Remove chicken and set aside on a plate.
2. Add the heavy cream, chicken broth, garlic powder, Italian seasoning, and parmesan cheese. Whisk over medium-high heat until it starts to thicken. Add the spinach and sundried tomatoes and let it simmer until the spinach begins to wilt. Add the chicken back to the pan and serve over pasta if desired.

Nutrition Per Serving: Calories: 434, Protein: 30 g, Fat: 31 g, Net Carbs: 3 g

Keto chicken enchilada bowl

TIME TO PREPARE
5 Minutes

COOK TIME
15 Minutes

Serving
4 People

INGREDIENTS

- Two tablespoon coconut oil (for searing chicken)
- 1 pound of boneless, skinless chicken thighs
- 3/4 cup (195g) red enchilada sauce
- 1/4 cup (60ml) water
- 1/4 cup (37g) chopped onion
- 1– 4 oz can dice green chiles

INSTRUCTIONS

1. In a pot or Dutch oven over medium heat, melt the coconut oil. Once hot, sear chicken thighs until lightly brown.
2. Pour in enchilada sauce and water, then add onion and green chiles. Reduce heat to a simmer and cover. Cook chicken for 17-25 minutes or until chicken is tender and fully cooked through at least 165 degrees internal temperature.
3. Carefully removes the chicken and place it onto a work surface. Chop or shred chicken (your preference), then add it back into the pot. Let the chicken simmer uncovered for an additional 10 minutes to absorb flavor and allow the sauce to reduce a little.
4. To serve, top with avocado, cheese, jalapeno, sour cream, tomato, and any other desired toppings. Feel free to customize these to your preference. If desired, serve alone or over cauliflower rice; just be sure to update your nutrition info as needed.

Nutrition Per Serving: Calories: 568, Protein: 38.3 g, Fat: 40.5 g, Net Carbs: 7 g

Jimmy Walnut Cookies

TIME TO PREPARE
10 Minutes

COOK TIME
60 Minutes

Serving
15 Cookies

INGREDIENTS

- Two cups (225g) almond flour (fine).
- One large egg (whisked).
- ½ cup (125g) butter (salted, softened).
- ⅔ cup (67g) erythritol (powder).
- ⅓ cup (40g) walnuts (finely chopped).

- 5 tbsp strawberry jam.
- 1 tsp vanilla extract.
- ½ tsp baking powder.
- Pinch of salt.

INSTRUCTIONS

1. Preheat the oven to 190 degrees.
2. In a large bowl, mix egg, almond flour, butter, baking powder, erythritol, vanilla extract, and salt; mix well until a dough is formed.
3. Place chopped walnuts on a plate. Roll the dough into 1 ½ inch balls and roll them in the walnuts to coat them.
4. Line a baking tray with greaseproof paper and bake cookies for 8-10 minutes.
5. Remove from the oven and make a small indent in the middle; place 1 tsp of jam in the indent and bake for an additional 10-12 minutes.
6. Place cookies on a rack and allow to cool for 30-40 minutes.

Nutrition Per Cookies: Calories: 163, Protein: 4 g, Fat: 17.3 g, Net Carbs: 4 g

Coconut & Nut Cookie Crumbles

TIME TO PREPARE
10 Minutes

COOK TIME
40 Minutes

Serving
12 Cookies

INGREDIENTS

- Two large egg yolks.
- ½ cup (60g) walnuts (finely chopped).
- ½ cup (85g) of chocolate chips (sugar-free).
- ½ cup (60g) of coconut flakes (unsweetened).

- ¼ cup (25g) erythritol.
- 2 tbsp coconut cream.
- 2 tbsp butter.

INSTRUCTIONS

1. Preheat the oven to 175 degrees.
2. In a large bowl, mix cream and butter until smooth.
3. Whisk in the egg yolks and erythritol and mix until well combined; mix in the remaining ingredients.
4. Line a baking tray with greaseproof paper; scoop 12 separate spoons of cookie mixture onto the tray, slightly flatten to form 12 cookies.
5. Bake for 18-20 minutes until golden brown.

Nutrition Per Serving: Calories: 119, Protein: 3.3 g, Fat: 12.5 g, Net Carbs: 3 g

Beautiful Blueberry Cookies

TIME TO PREPARE
10 Minutes

COOK TIME
30 Minutes

Serving
12 Cookies

INGREDIENTS

- One large egg.
- 1 ½ cups (160g) almond flour.
- ¾ cup (75g) erythritol (granulated).
- ½ cup (120g) butter (melted).
- ½ cup (75g) blueberries (frozen).

- 1 tsp vanilla extract.
- ½ tsp xanthan gum.
- ½ tsp baking powder.
- ¼ tsp salt.

INSTRUCTIONS

1. Preheat the oven to 175 degrees.
2. In a bowl, mix erythritol and butter until well combined; stir in egg and vanilla.
3. Whisk in almond flour, xanthan gum, baking powder, and salt; gently fold in the blueberries.
4. Line a baking sheet with greaseproof paper and scoop 12 balls from the cookie mixture, place on the sheet.
5. Bake for 15-18 minutes until golden brown.

Nutrition Per Cookies: Calories: 98, Protein: 1 g, Fat: 11.5 g, Net Carbs: 2 g

Chicken and Snap

TIME TO PREPARE
5 Minutes

COOK TIME
15 Minutes

Serving
4 People

INGREDIENTS

- Two tablespoons vegetable oil
- One bunch scallions, thinly sliced
- Two garlic cloves, minced
- One red bell pepper, thinly sliced
- 2½ cups (170g) snap peas
- 1¼ cups (180g) boneless skinless chicken breast, thinly sliced
- Salt and freshly ground Black Pepper

- Three tablespoons soy sauce
- Two tablespoons rice vinegar
- Two teaspoons Sriracha (optional)
- Two tablespoons sesame seeds, plus more for finishing
- Three tablespoons chopped fresh cilantro, plus more for finishing

INSTRUCTIONS

1. In a large sauté pan, heat the oil over medium heat. Add the scallions and garlic, and sauté until fragrant, about 1 minute. Add the bell pepper and snap peas and sauté until just tender, 2 to 3 minutes.
2. Add the chicken and cook until it is golden and fully cooked, and the vegetables are tender for 4 to 5 minutes.
3. Add the soy sauce, rice vinegar, Sriracha (if using), and sesame seeds; toss well to combine. Allow the mixture to simmer for 1 to 2 minutes.
4. Stir in the cilantro, then garnish with a sprinkle of extra cilantro and sesame seeds. Serve immediately.

Nutrition Per Serving: Calories: 288, Protein: 24 g, Fat: 11.5 g, Net Carbs: 10 g

Chewy Seeded Chocolate-Chip Cookies

TIME TO PREPARE
5 Minutes

COOK TIME
15 Minutes

Serving
30 Cookies

INGREDIENTS

- One large egg.
- One cup (130g) sunflower seed butter.
- ¾ cup (95g) Swerve (granulated).

- 2 tbsp chocolate chips (sugar-free).
- 1 tsp baking powder.

INSTRUCTIONS

1. Preheat the oven to 175 degrees.
2. In a large bowl, mix all ingredients until well combined.
3. Line a baking sheet with greaseproof paper.
4. Using a tablespoon, spoon out 30 balls of cookie dough and space out across the baking sheet.
5. Bake for 12-15 minutes until browned. Allow cooling for five minutes.

Nutrition Per Cookies: Calories: 67, Protein: 3 g, Fat: 6 g, Net Carbs: 3 g

Perfectly Proud Pumpkin Cookies

TIME TO PREPARE
5 Minutes

COOK TIME
30 Minutes

Serving
22 People

INGREDIENTS

- 7 oz almond flour.
- 4 oz melted butter (unsalted).
- One large egg.

- 2 oz erythritol.
- 2 tsp pumpkin spice mix.
- 4 drops pumpkin extract.

INSTRUCTIONS

1. Preheat the oven to 160 degrees.
2. In a large bowl, mix almond flour, erythritol, and pumpkin spice mix until well combined.
3. Stir in egg, butter, and pumpkin extract until a sticky dough is formed.
4. Using a tbsp, make 22 balls and flatten each one on a greased baking tray.
5. Bake for 25-30 until golden and crispy.
6. Allow cooling.

Nutrition Per Serving: Calories: 95, Protein: 3 g, Fat: 10 g, Net Carbs: 2 g

Chilli avocado

TIME TO PREPARE
5 Minutes

COOK TIME
0 Minutes

Serving
1 People

INGREDIENTS

- ½ small avocado
- ¼ tsp chilli flakes
- juice of ¼ lime

INSTRUCTIONS

1. Sprinkle the avocado with the chilli flakes, lime juice and a little black pepper, and eat with a spoon.

Nutrition Per Serving: Calories: 102, Protein: 1 g, Fat: 11 g, Net Carbs: 0.5 g

Creamy Keto Chicken Casserole

TIME TO PREPARE
10 Minutes

COOK TIME
30 Minutes

Serving
4 People

INGREDIENTS

- 32 oz chicken thighs (boneless and skinless).
- 16 oz cauliflower (florets).
- 7 oz cheddar cheese (grated).
- 4 oz cherry tomatoes (halved).
- 1 ½ oz butter.
- One leek (chopped).

- ¾ cup (180g) sour cream.
- ½ cup (112g) of cream cheese (softened).
- 3 tbsp pesto.
- 3 tbsp lemon juice (fresh).
- ½ tsp black pepper.

INSTRUCTIONS

1. Preheat oven at 400 degrees.
2. In a large frying pan, melt the butter and fry chicken until cooked and golden brown.
3. In a bowl, mix sour cream, cream cheese, lemon juice, pesto, and Pepper until well combined.
4. Place chicken in a large ovenproof dish, pour cream cheese mixture on top.
5. Add cauliflower, leek, and tomatoes.
6. Bake in the oven for 25 minutes, remove and sprinkle cheese on top.
7. Bake for a further 10 minutes or until cheese is melted and golden brown.

Nutrition Per Serving: Calories: 557, Protein: 34 g, Fat: 24.5 g, Net Carbs: 0.31 g

Coconut Crunch Cookie

TIME TO PREPARE
10 Minutes

COOK TIME
35 Minutes

Serving
18 People

INGREDIENTS

- 3 oz desiccated coconut.
- Three large egg whites.
- ¼ cup (25g) erythritol.
- 12 drop liquid Stevia.
- 3 tbsp butter (melted).

INSTRUCTIONS

1. Preheat the oven to 150 degrees.
2. In a large bowl, mix egg whites, coconut, erythritol, and liquid Stevia until well combined.
3. Stir in the melted butter.
4. On a baking sheet lined with greaseproof paper, make 18 tablespoon-sized balls; flatten each one.
5. Bake for 20-25 minutes until browned and crisp.
6. Allow cooling.

Nutrition Per Serving: Calories: 59, Protein: 3 g, Fat: 10.5 g, Net Carbs: 2 g

Low Carb Cauliflower Breadsticks

TIME TO PREPARE
10 Minutes

COOK TIME
15 Minutes

Serving
2 People

INGREDIENTS

- One head cauliflower raw
- 1/2 cup (112.5g) Mozzarella Cheese shredded
- 1/2 cup (50g) Parmesan cheese shaved
- One large egg
- 1/2 tablespoon garlic minced
- 1/2 tablespoon fresh basil chopped
- 1/2 tablespoon fresh Italian flat-leaf parsley chopped
- One teaspoon salt
- 1/2 teaspoon ground black pepper
- 3/4 cup (170g) Mozzarella Cheese shredded

INSTRUCTIONS

1. Preheat oven to 425°F and line a baking sheet with parchment paper or a silicone baking mat.
2. Rice the cauliflower by coring it and breaking it into florets. Then place it in the bowl of a food processor and pulse until it is the texture of rice. (If your cauliflower seems excessively moist, squeeze the riced, raw cauliflower in a paper towel to help remove moisture.)
3. In a large bowl, mix the riced cauliflower, 1/2 cup shredded Mozzarella cheese, 1/2 cup Parmesan cheese, one egg, 1/2 tablespoon fresh garlic, 1/2 tablespoon fresh basil, 1/2 tablespoon fresh parsley, one teaspoon salt, and 1/2 teaspoon black pepper until combined and holds together. Place the mixture onto the lined baking sheet and spread out into a rectangle about 9x7" and 1/4" thick.
4. Bake in the preheated oven for 10-12 minutes. Remove from oven and top with 3/4 cup shredded Mozzarella cheese and return to oven to continue baking until the cheese is melted and starting to brown. Cool about 10 minutes and cut into 'breadsticks.' Garnish with fresh herbs and Parmesan cheese. Serve with your favourite Red Sauce and enjoy!

Nutrition Per Serving: Calories: 143, Protein: 11 g, Fat: 5 g, Net Carbs: 2 g

Shrimp & Sausage Skillet Paleo

TIME TO PREPARE
10 Minutes

COOK TIME
20 Minutes

Serving
3 People

INGREDIENTS

- 1 lb of medium or large shrimp (peeled and deveined)
- 6 oz of pre-cooked smoked sausage, chopped (choose your favourite)
- 3/4 cup (112g) diced red bell pepper
- 3/4 cup (112g) diced green bell pepper
- 1/2 of a medium yellow onion, diced
- 1/4 cup (60g) chicken stock

- One zucchini, chopped
- Two garlic cloves, diced
- Salt & Pepper to taste
- Pinch of red pepper flakes
- 2 tsp Old Bay Seasoning
- Olive oil or coconut oil
- Optional garnish: chopped parsley

INSTRUCTIONS

1. Heat a large skillet over medium-high heat with some olive oil or coconut oil
2. Season shrimp with Old Bay Seasoning
3. Cook shrimp about 3-4 minutes until opaque – remove and set aside
4. Cook onions and bell peppers in skillet with 2 Tbsp of olive oil or coconut oil for about 2 minutes
5. Add sausage and zucchini to the skillet, cook another 2 minutes
6. Put cooked shrimp back into the skillet along with the garlic, and cook everything for about 1 minute

7. Pour chicken stock into the pan and mix through to moisten everything
8. Add salt, ground pepper, and red pepper flakes to taste
9. Remove from heat, garnish with parsley and serve hot

Nutrition Per Serving: Calories: 750, Protein: 17 g, Fat: 32 g, Net Carbs: 7 g

Salmon Rolls with Lemon Sauce

TIME TO PREPARE
10 Minutes

COOK TIME
20 Minutes

Serving
2 People

INGREDIENTS

- 4 (5 ounces) salmon fillets, skins removed
- salt and Pepper to taste
- 1 (12 ounces) container ricotta
- 1/2 cup Parmigiano Reggiano (parmesan), grated
- Two tablespoons basil, chopped

- Two teaspoons lemon zest
- salt and Pepper to taste
- 1/2 pound asparagus, trimmed
- One tablespoon butter
- 1/2 cup chicken broth
- Two tablespoons lemon juice
- Two teaspoons cornstarch

INSTRUCTIONS

1. Season the salmon fillets with salt and Pepper to taste, lay them down with the skin side up, top with the mixture of the ricotta, parmesan, basil, lemon zest, salt and Pepper, several spears of asparagus and roll them up before placing them on a greased baking sheet with the seam side down.
2. Bake in a preheated 425F/220C oven until the salmon is just cooked, about 15-20 minutes.
3. Meanwhile, melt the butter in a small saucepan over medium heat, add the mixture of the broth, lemon juice, and corn starch and heat until it thickens, about 3-5 minutes.
4. Serve the salmon rolls topped with the lemon sauce and optionally garnish with more basil and lemon zest.

Nutrition Per Serving: Calories: 400.5, Protein: 14.3 g, Fat: 38.9 g, Net Carbs: 8.1 g

Creamy Chicken Chasseur

TIME TO PREPARE
10 Minutes

COOK TIME
15 Minutes

Serving
4 People

INGREDIENTS

- 16 oz chicken breast.
- 8 oz baby mushrooms.
- Four cloves garlic (crushed).
- ½ red onion (finely chopped).
- 1 ½ cups thick cream.
- ¼ cup parmesan (grated).

- 2 tbsp butter (unsalted).
- 1 tbsp olive oil.
- 1 tsp mixed herbs (dried).
- 1 tsp garlic powder.
- ¼ tsp salt.
- ¼ tsp black pepper.

INSTRUCTIONS

1. Slice chicken breasts in half (lengthways), making them easier to cook.
2. In a bowl, mix garlic powder, mixed herbs, salt, and Pepper. Season both sides of chicken breasts with the mixture.
3. In a large frying pan, melt the butter. Fry the chicken breasts, 5 minutes on each side or until thoroughly cooked. Set cooked chicken to one side.
4. Using the same frying pan, add mushrooms and onion; fry until tender and slightly browned. Add crushed garlic and cook for an additional minute.
5. Reduce heat and stir in the thick cream, parmesan, and herbs; simmer until sauce begins to thicken, stirring continuously.
6. Return chicken and any juices back to the pan, cook for an additional 3-4 minutes.

Nutrition Per Serving: Calories: 570, Protein: 48.3 g, Fat: 31.9 g, Net Carbs: 7 g

Garlic Butter Brazilian Steak Recipe

TIME TO PREPARE
10 Minutes

COOK TIME
10 Minutes

Serving
4 People

INGREDIENTS

- Six medium cloves garlic
- kosher salt
- 1.5 lb. skirt steak, trimmed and cut into four pieces
- freshly ground Black Pepper

- Two tablespoons canola oil or vegetable oil
- 2 oz. unsalted butter (4 tablespoons)
- One tablespoon chopped fresh flat-leaf parsley

INSTRUCTIONS

1. Peel the garlic cloves and smash them with the side of a chef's knife. Sprinkle the garlic lightly with salt and mince it.
2. Pat the steak dry and season generously on both sides with salt and Pepper. In a heavy-duty 12-inch skillet, heat the oil over medium-high heat until shimmering hot.

Add the steak and brown well on both sides, 2 to 3 minutes per side for medium-rare. Transfer the steak to a plate and let rest while you make the garlic butter.

3. In an 8-inch skillet, melt the butter over low heat. Add the garlic and cook, swirling the pan frequently, until lightly golden, about 4 minutes. Lightly salt to taste.
4. Slice the steak, if you like, and transfer to 4 plates. Spoon the garlic butter over the steak, sprinkle with the parsley, and serve.

Nutrition Per Serving: Calories: 538, Protein: 18.1 g, Fat: 31.7 g, Net Carbs: 2 g

Keto Chocolate Heaven

TIME TO PREPARE
10 Minutes

COOK TIME
30 Minutes

Serving
15 Slices

INGREDIENTS

- 300 g (10.5 oz) 70% chocolate
- 175 g (6 oz) butter
- 2 teaspoon vanilla extract
- 6 eggs - medium

- 6 tablespoon single or heavy whipping cream
- 4 teaspoon granulated sweetener of choice or more, to your taste

INSTRUCTIONS

1. Melt the chocolate and butter together over a low heat in a saucepan. Remove from the heat and allow to cool slightly before adding the vanilla extract.
2. In another bowl beat the eggs, cream and sweetener together for 3-4 minutes (use a stick blender or hand whisk). It will go frothy and remain runny.
3. Slowly add the egg mixture to the chocolate mixture in the saucepan, stirring all the time. As you add more egg mixture, the chocolate and butter will thicken to the consistency of custard.
4. Pour into a prepared tin. Grease a loose bottom cake tin with butter then line the loose bottom with baking paper and push through the outer ring so the baking paper adds a seal and stops the cake mixture from leaking.
5. Bake at 180C/ 350F for 20 - 30 minutes, or more depending on your oven. Bake until it is just set in the centre, do not overcook the cake.

Nutrition Per Slice: Calories: 250, Protein: 4 g, Fat: 21 g, Net Carbs: 7 g

CONCLUSION

One of the primary keys to any successful diet or lifestyle change has always been the recipes that fit in with the principles of the diet. I am sure there are many ways to achieve ketosis and to attain that weight loss goal. However, you do not want to get there by just having the same old dishes over and over again.

Variety is the name of the game here, which is crucial in ensuring the sustainability of the ketogenic diet. With the flavorful and delicious recipes found in this step by step keto cookbook, they will be useful additions for any keto dieter at any stage of their ketogenic journey. I have yet to see anyone complain about having too many easy yet delicious recipes!

ONE LAST THING...

If you enjoyed this book or found it useful, I'd be very grateful if you'd post a short review on Amazon. Your support really does make a difference, and I read all the reviews personally so I can get your feedback and make this book even better.

Thanks, again for your support!